40 HADITH on COMMUNITY SERVICE & ACTIVISM

Dr. Mohannad Hakeem

KUBE
PUBLISHING

40 Hadith of Community Service and Activism

First published in England by
Kube Publishing Ltd,
Markfield Conference Centre,
Ratby Lane, Markfield,
Leicestershire, LE67 9SY,
United Kingdom Tel: +44 (0) 1530 249230

Website: www.kubepublishing.com
Email: info@kubepublishing.com

Cataloguing-in-Publication Data is available from the British Library

ISBN Paperback: 978-1-84774-159-2
ISBN Ebook: 978-1-84774-160-8

Cover Design: Jannah Haque
Internal Design and Typesetting: Nasir Cadir
Chapter Illustrations: Bloom Graphics Design Studio
Printer: IMAK, Turkey

CONTENTS

DEDICATION

YOUNG ACTIVISTS, campus student organizations, and local institutions spearheading various initiatives and programmes for the betterment of our collective wellbeing and future—this one is for you.

Khaṭībs searching for a relevant hadith for that upcoming *khuṭbah*, motivational speakers seeking prophetic guidance for their next audience, and all of us entrusted with providing our communities understanding and hope, particularly in times of turbulence and trials—this is also for you.

The men and women behind the scenes in every community, sacrificing their weekends, family time, and money to keep things running at each mosque despite criticism and lack of resources; executive committees; educational and outreach committees; and yes, even *masjid* board members—this is for you too.

Our esteemed social experts and researchers responsible for finding the root causes of our community issues, shouldered with the responsibility of keeping us informed—this may be of help to you.

Last but not least: friends, allies, and fellow activists from every community and walk of life; men and women who believe in the power of the people, and are searching for universal wisdom and values to help reach true success—this is one to add to your shelf.

Dr Mohannad Hakeem
Dearborn, Michigan
Rabīʿ al-Thānī, 1443 AH,
November 2021

In the Name of Allah, the Most Compassionate, the Ever-Merciful

FOREWORD

IN AN ERA OF confusion, doubts, and subjective truths, the Muslim community is in need of consistent guidance, education, and awareness about the correct application of Islam in their respective societies. One of the greatest tools available to every Muslim is a framework that establishes the foundation of Truth in a clear and concise manner, particularly with community service, civic engagement, and activism.

Activism, in its numerous meanings, cannot be complete or correct if it is guided by anything other than Islam. All human beings believe in a moral reference point, be that objective *or* subjective, and Muslims are undoubtedly required to serve the Creator and His creation via the Islamic paradigm, one that is established upon the Qur'an and authentic hadith. Oftentimes, Muslim beliefs in Western nations are shaped by their local predominant ideology, which has the potential to distort their worldview. A lens shaped by a liberal philosophy, for instance, has the potential to cause Muslims to engage in everyday matters—including community service and activism—in a manner that is considered prohibited in Islam, and one that inevitably harms present society and its future by preventing those Muslims from using the actual solutions that Islam provides.

In this important and timeless manuscript, Dr Mohannad strategically compiled and commented upon forty significant prophetic narrations to establish a clear framework for all Muslims, particularly in Western nations, and especially those interested or engaged in community service and activism.

Every hadith included in this compilation can be expanded upon in more detail, but the author—in a calculated manner, may Allah bless him—has condensed and clarified the most important details every Muslim needs and presented them alongside each hadith in the text. The compilation has been written in a very practical, coherent manner to benefit all readers, young and old, with a breakdown of peoples' motivations, clarity on what they are pursuing, etiquette and methodology, the *fiqh* of activism, and a guide for self-care. This compilation has the potential to benefit countless Muslims for generations to come, by the will of Allah, to be translated into numerous languages, and to be studied and commented on by people of all knowledges in a timeless manner. Furthermore, for many Muslims today, an Islamic framework and a strengthening of their beliefs protects them against an inferiority complex when engaging in social justice causes, religious dialogue, and ethical dilemmas.

Additionally, the framework of activism via the lens of Islam undoubtedly brings benefit to countless non-Muslims interested in understanding Islam and its role in society. Moreover, for non-Muslims, there is the tremendous benefit of understanding how Muslims view community service and activism and how to engage with Muslims on various causes without expecting them to compromise on their beliefs and moral values.

Ultimately, society does not change overnight, and the night is always replaced with a new day; the Muslim who strives to change the world should see every morning as a new opportunity and understand that every generation will die and be replaced by another. Gradual, structural, global change requires multi-generational sincerity, wisdom, strategy, knowledge, implementation, and perseverance, leaving the results to the One who knows all things. With the limited time we have in this world, and with the Light of Truth in our hearts, we cannot afford to be ignorant about these crucial prophetic narrations and how to implement them in our respective societies.

May Allah bless and reward the author of this text and all of its contributors, and guide all of its readers to sincere and impactful change around the world.

Suleiman Hani
November 29, 2021

PREFACE

IMAGINE A WORLD where the hadith of Prophet Muhammad, may Allah bless him and give him peace, are featured in major news headlines and media outlets. Imagine a new generation of volunteers, community organizers and activists who quote Prophet Muhammad's words in their meetings, marketing material and rhetoric. Imagine teachers, authors, artists, and policy makers all reaching out to his wisdom for solution and guidance. If you are excited about being part of such a vision, then this book is a stepping stone for making that vision a reality.

Since the start of the twenty-first century, the rise of anti-Islamic bigotry, or what is commonly referred to as Islamophobia, has pushed Muslim minorities in the West towards activism and civic engagement. Whether manifested in rallying to raise awareness on social justice issues, organizing campaigns for political candidates, or running online fundraisers, Muslims continue to significantly influence this sphere of work. This has been accompanied by multiple calls for positive integration of Muslims in their respective communities through service and charity.

Like any other group, Muslims are expected to voice their concerns, work passionately for their issues, and leave a positive legacy wherever they go. They could be doing so from a position of being marginalized and oppressed but also from a position of being strong and prosperous. However, activism and service in the Muslim community must not be merely reactive to world events. As Muslims, our actions are manifestations of the firm values of our faith. Those values are consistent principles that we are obliged to uphold if we want to achieve peace and justice. In other words, being a productive member of society is a Divine duty before being a civic one. With the right intention and execution, it is an act of worship that–by the will of God–we can find on our scale on the Day of Judgement. Thus, it is imperative that our involvement in such fields follow the noble and Divine legislation: the Qur'anic principles and the tradition of our beloved Prophet Muhammad, may Allah bless him and give him peace.

This book is a collection of hadith, narrated teachings and actions from the Prophet Muhammad, may Allah bless him and give him peace, that try to build such a framework. While the hadith themselves are not specifically limited to the scope of this book, they can inspire, inform and guide in ways most pleasing to Allah and His Messenger. This collection is written with an international audience in mind as the Prophet Muhammad's teachings provide universal principles for all those who wish to be agents of change and make a difference. A world like ours is in dire need of the timeless principles taught by the man who was Divinely sent as a mercy to all mankind. This collection contains glimpses of his prophetic guidance and wisdom for us to be able to draw both inspiration and instruction to guide our most passionate social work. Each hadith is supplemented with a commentary as well as actionable items that bring prophetic teachings to the lived world of the Muslim activist and community organizer.

INTRODUCTION

COMMUNITY SERVICE and activism are deeply rooted in our Islamic tradition. Such modern society's definitions of leaving an impact or calling for social justice resonate with multiple genuine Islamic terms. The different forms of charity, serving people, and fulfilling their needs (*qaḍā' ḥawā'ij al-nās*) are manifestations of social activism. In the educational sphere, this may be considered as a form of preaching Islam (delivering *da'wah*), outreach, educating Muslims and non-Muslims, and raising awareness about a cause. In terms of political activism, we see the notions of enjoining good and forbidding evil (*al-amr bi'l-ma'rūf wa'l-nahy 'an al-munkar*), speaking truth to power, and giving advice (*naṣīḥah*) to the ruler and to the public. Without getting stuck on terminologies and nomenclature, this book defines God-centred activism and service to include activities such as:

- Volunteering at a local soup kitchen.
- Representing Islam at college campuses (at the Muslim Students' Association, for example) and in employee resource groups (such as the Inter Faith Network).
- Mentoring a youth group at a school or summer camp.
- Raising funds to help the needy.
- Researching ways to define our priorities and improve our operations and our service.
- Establishing institutions and building communities to ensure the longevity and sustainability of our activities and our projects.
- Mobilizing communities and campaigning towards spiritual, social, and eventual political change.
- Voter registration drives and raising awareness about a community's rights and responsibilities.
- Opposition to a policy through boycotting, lobbying, protesting, and any form of expression that is granted by law.

It is important to note that the word *activist* has more far-reaching implications nowadays than its traditional context of political activism and advocacy. For Muslim minorities living in the Western hemisphere, this is particularly true in the age of Islamophobia. The circle of activists has expanded to include the woman who wears the hijab as she is shopping at the local grocery store, and the young Muslim man in secondary school who does not have a girlfriend and must explain himself to his peers. It also includes self-proclaimed non-religious Muslims who are proud of their Muslim heritage and feel the need to represent their Islamic faith within their social circles. Many of these activists have common traits that transcend generations, ethnic groups, and social classes. They cherish the heritage and the group identity that Islam brings to their lives, even if they fall short in understanding or applying some of its teachings. They are motivated to represent their faith in the best way possible and to spend their free time in volunteering at events.

INTELLECTUAL CHALLENGES FACING MUSLIM ACTIVISTS

Clearly, the above-mentioned manifestations of activism and service are deeply rooted within the Islamic tradition. However, Muslims living in Western democracies have felt uncomfortable about some aspects of their political engagement, for fear of compromising some elements of their faith. As an example, at the time this book was written, most American Muslims have been politically aligned with far-left progressive movements. Those parties have generally protected Muslim rights of worship and institution building, and fought hard for the inclusion of all elements of the American society. However, the same parties who may be our allies in protecting rights of worship (at least in some countries and under some conditions) may also promote a morality and lifestyles that go against traditional Islamic values. Being relatively new to the political arena, our community has to yet find a sound balance in maintaining both ends of the equation: to stay deeply rooted in the Islamic tradition while at the same time having clear and unambiguous stances on social justice issues.

THE IMPORTANCE OF CONTEXTUALIZING THE MUSLIM TRADITION

Throughout the life of Prophet Muhammad, may Allah bless him and give him peace, early Muslims experienced different political and social circumstances. Beginning as a persecuted minority in the Makkan period, to holding refugee status in Abyssinia, to becoming a minority in a multi-faith community during the early years in Madinah, and then finally building a strong government that engaged in war and peace-making with neighbouring tribes in the later Madinan period.

This plethora of examples and situations provides guidelines for the Muslim community in various contexts and under different conditions. The Qur'an provides a huge amount of history and stories of previous prophets, all of whom had a variety of experiences. Some ruled large kingdoms, such as Sulaymān and Dāwūd, while others, like Musa and Ibrahim, lived as refugees for most of their lives. The Prophet Muhammad himself, may Allah bless him and give him peace, drew inspiration from stories of previous prophets at the appropriate time, and we should consequently follow the same approach. Clearly, this compilation of hadith does not apply only to activism, but can be considered foundational hadith from which activists can derive benefit, while keeping the following applications in mind:

- Maximizing the potential of individuals, communities, and civic society (rather than governments or large institutions).
- Working within societies that promote freedom of speech and ensure basic human rights.

- Working within one's circle of influence (your own self, and those around you) to affect one's circle of concern (wars, poverty, Islamophobia, and other external factors).

CALL TO ACTION

This collection of forty hadith is meant to serve as a 'Muslim's handbook on how to change the world'. To do so, it is ideal that you start your journey with the correct intent and mindset, and ask yourself:

- Are you ready to dive into timeless wisdom and hit the ground running with such wisdom?
- Are you ready for a well-rounded dose of spirituality, service, activism, leadership, self-help, and thought-provoking insight? All from prophetic wisdom?
- Are you ready to immerse yourself into scholarly commentaries and discussions, all packaged in a relatively short and relatable read?
- Are you excited about sharing the universal wisdom of Prophet Muhammad's words with your non-Muslim allies and colleagues?
- Are you willing to influence your people and drive your organization towards success from the words of the man who has achieved unmatched worldly success, even according to some people who did not choose to follow him?
- Are you interested to decipher the terms and definitions that you have heard over and over in those endless discussions on what's permissible or not in political activism?

If your answer to any or all of these questions was yes, then this book is meant for you, and you are meant to experience this collection of forty hadith.

You may choose to read this book in its entirety, skim chapters and hadith in order to examine a title of particular interest, or just browse through the table of contents to get an idea of the topics covered. You may have liked to see other hadith included, or disagreed with the commentary or placement of certain hadith within a given context. After all, this compilation is an attempt to bring Muslim community workers and activists towards a unified framework that is based on timeless principles from our beloved Prophet, may Allah bless him and give him peace. We are trying to answer the most pertinent questions that every Muslim activist should ask themselves:

- Why did I choose this line of work as a way of life? Chapter 1.
- What are the community service activities that Prophet Muhammad (may Allah bless him and send him peace) expects from me? Chapter 2.
- What is expected from my involvement in politics as a Muslim? Chapter 3.
- Who should I look for, hire, train, and retain in my team and my organization? Chapter 4.
- How should I carry myself in my activism work? Chapter 5.
- How can I make sure that I do not cross the boundaries of Islam in my political activism? Chapter 6.
- While being involved in my activism and community service, how can I take care of myself and ensure that I don't get burnt out?

CHAPTER 1

THE WHY

THE SPIRITUALITY OF AN ACTIVIST

THE FIRST QUESTION that Muslim activists and community workers should ask themselves is *why*. *Why* did I choose to volunteer for this event or that cause? Clearly, volunteering does not involve getting paid, while activism goes beyond that to include multiple layers of risks and challenges.

One could find multiple reasons to join this line of work, such as a personal experience that may have shaped our worldview, or an inherited passion from a family member towards a certain cause. For a Muslim, such reasons are valid as long as they fit under the umbrella of seeking to please

Allah. A sincere intention is what causes our deeds to either be accepted and heavily rewarded by the Almighty, or otherwise rejected due to other worldly desires, such as showing off or seeking praise from people. In Surah *al-Insān*, Allah describes what the intention behind every act of service, for a believer should be:

> **And they give food in spite of love for it to the needy, the orphan, and the captive; they tell them: 'We feed you only for the countenance of Allah. We wish not from you reward or gratitude. Indeed, we fear from our Lord a Day austere and distressful.' So Allah will protect them from the evil of that Day and give them radiance and happiness. And will reward them for what they patiently endured with a garden in Paradise and silk garments.** (al-Insān 76: 8–12)

The spirituality of activism starts with the *why* question, from having pure intentions, and continues to accompany us throughout our whole journey. It ensures that the *how* (the qualities and values that we adopt) and the *what* (the services that we offer) are also aligned with the *why*, or what pleases Allah. In addition, answering *why* helps a group to refine its mission, vision and metrics of success. It helps us consider both the spiritual and the material dimensions when defining and refining our *why*. For example: we can write a personal or a group slogan, goal, and *why* as follows: 'When I (we) meet Allah, I (we) want to be proud of ...'.

HADITH 1
BEGIN WITH THE VERY END IN MIND

إنَّما الأعمالُ بالنِّيَّاتِ وإنَّما لِكلِّ امرئٍ ما نوى فمن كانت هجرتُهُ إلى اللَّهِ ورسولِهِ فَ
هجرتُهُ إلى اللَّهِ ورسولِهِ ومن كانت هجرتُهُ إلى دنيا يصيبُها أو امرأةٍ ينْكحُها فَهجر
تُهُ إلى ما هاجرَ إليْهِ (البخاري و مسلم)

'Umar ibn al-Khaṭṭāb (RA) narrated that the Messenger of Allah, may Allah bless him and give him peace, said:Deeds are bound by the intentions behind them, and each person will be rewarded according to his intention. So, whoever migrated for the sake of Allah and His Messenger, then his migration will be accepted as one for the sake of Allah and His Messenger; and whoever migrated for worldly benefits or for a woman to marry, then his migration would be rewarded based on what he migrated for. (Bukhārī and Muslim)

COMMENTARY

This hadith has always been the introductory hadith to most of the 40 hadith collections compiled by our scholars, such as the famous 40 hadith collection by Imam Nawawī. This comes as no surprise as having a pure intention to please Allah should be the foundation of every Muslim's deeds and actions. In this worldly life, a pure intention is the only way to keep oneself motivated in tough times and stay humble in moments of glory and success. In the Hereafter, a pure intention is one of the main reasons for why some deeds are rewarded by Allah multiple times, up to 700 times, while others are considered worthless and of no value.

For Muslim activists, we begin every deed by considering the *very* end in mind, which is the moment we shall meet our Lord and present our deeds on the Day of Judgement. The 'end' is not when we raise our first million, get a plaque to honour our contributions, or open another branch of our organization. While these may be decent milestones and opportunities to celebrate success, the real celebration for a Muslim is the moment of meeting Allah, in the hope that the worship and the service that he or she offered will be accepted. This sincerity check should be done before, during, and after the action. An early scholar, Yūsuf ibn al-Ḥusayn, used to say:

> 'Sincerity is the rarest commodity in this world, and many times I try to remove the thought of showing off from my heart, but it feels like it keeps growing inside my heart in a different format and colour.'[1]

The Messenger of Allah, may Allah bless him and give him peace, mentioned on another occasion how certain individuals who did honourable deeds with the wrong intentions will be held accountable and even punished for them on the Day of Judgement.

Abū Hurayrah relates that the Messenger of Allah, may Allah bless him and give him peace, said:

> *Verily, the first of the people to be judged on the Day of Resurrection will be a man who was martyred. He will be brought forth for Judgement and reminded of all the blessings*

1 Ibn Qayyim al-Jawziyah, *Madarij al-salikin.*

> *that Allah has bestowed upon him, and he will acknowledge them all. Allah will ask: 'What did you do about them?' The man will reply: 'I fought in Your cause until I was martyred.' Allah will respond: 'You have lied, for you fought only so it would be said you were brave, and thus it was said.' Then, Allah will order him to be dragged on his face until he is cast into Hellfire.'* (Muslim)

The hadith goes on to describe two other individuals: a charitable person who donated a lot of money, and a teacher of the Qur'an who taught it to the masses. Unfortunately, both have done such deeds with the wrong intentions. According to the hadith, such corrupt and insincere intentions caused all three to be held accountable and even punished instead of being rewarded.

SUGGESTED ACTION ITEMS

1. It helps if you keep a private journal to document and reflect on your intentions and your deeds. Write your intentions behind all the activities that you engage in, and use your imagination to describe your dreams, expectations, and spiritual benefits from your community involvement. By the same token, reflect on and write down how regretful you would be if such intentions were not purely for the sake of Allah. Try to be as specific and descriptive as possible, instead of using a generic in the way of Allah (*fī sabīl Allāh*) comment. For example, one could write:

'I am teaching this hadith to this group of students in the hope that it will inspire and influence their thoughts and actions as the exact words of the Prophet Muhammad, may Allah bless him and give him peace, influenced the Companions.'

2. This hadith inspires us to have the proper intention in everything we do, even beyond known acts of worship and community service. Muʿādh ibn Jabal once said, 'I hope to be rewarded for my sleep as much as I hope for the reward of getting up for the night prayer' (Bukhārī and Muslim). Ibn Ḥajar commented on this by saying, 'He seeks for the reward in his resting time as he seeks it for his hard work, because if the intention from rest is to strengthen one's commitment to worship, then the reward will be given.' [2]

   In addition, one could have multiple intentions behind each deed. Such an example is to pay charity for the sake of purifying one's money, softening the heart, helping a family in need, and maintaining the ties of kinship.

3. One could be sincerely working for the sake of Allah and receive some worldly materialistic rewards in return. We should not feel guilty when this

2 Ibn Hajar, *Fath al-Bari bi Sharh Sahih al-Bukhari*, (Dar Al-Risalah Al-Alamiyah , Beirut 2013).

happens, especially if we did not ask for worldly recognition or compensation. Abū Dharr reported that the Messenger, may Allah bless him and give him peace, was asked, 'What is your opinion about the person who has done good deeds while receiving praise from the people?' The Prophet said, 'It is the immediate glad tidings for a believer.' (Muslim)

Community workers who do not understand this subtle point may assume that Islam requires extreme selflessness from them; some may dissociate themselves from any positive feedback or worldly gains. This may work against human nature as a healthy dose of positive reinforcement might be needed to keep our motivation and direction. This can also result in either one of two extremes: either stopping the work altogether, or shifting their intention to solely seek people's praise. Also, we should differentiate between the different types of glad tidings that we receive. A praise of the likes of 'you're so amazing' is not the same as 'your good works have helped me become a better person'. The effect varies with the type of praise or encouragement offered.

HADITH 2
WORKING BEHIND THE SCENES

عَنْ أَبِي هُرَيْرَةَ، عَنِ النَّبِيِّ صلى الله عليه وسلم قَالَ ' تَعِسَ عَبْدُ الدِّينَارِ وَعَبْدُ الدِّرْهَمِ وَعَبْدُ الْخَمِيصَةِ، إِنْ أُعْطِيَ رَضِيَ، وَإِنْ لَمْ يُعْطَ سَخِطَ، تَعِسَ وَانْتَكَسَ، وَإِذَا شِيكَ فَلاَ انْتَقَشَ، طُوبَى لِعَبْدٍ آخِذٍ بِعِنَانِ فَرَسِهِ فِي سَبِيلِ اللَّهِ، أَشْعَثَ رَأْسُهُ مُغْبَرَّةٍ قَدَمَاهُ، إِنْ كَانَ فِي الْحِرَاسَةِ كَانَ فِي الْحِرَاسَةِ، وَإِنْ كَانَ فِي السَّاقَةِ كَانَ فِي السَّاقَةِ، إِنِ اسْتَأْذَنَ لَمْ يُؤْذَنْ لَهُ، وَإِنْ شَفَعَ لَمْ يُشَفَّعْ (البخاري)

Abū Hurayrah reported that the Prophet Muhammad, may Allah bless him and give him peace, said:

Wretched is the slave of gold, silver, and fine clothes. If he is given, he is pleased, but if he is not given, he is displeased. May he perish and relapse, and if he is pierced with a thorn, may this thorn stay in his body forever! May Allah bless with Paradise another slave, who holds the reins of his horse to strive in the path of God, with his hair unkempt and feet covered with dust. The one who, if appointed in the vanguard, he is perfectly satisfied with his post of guarding, and if he is appointed at the rear of the army, he is fine with his position. He is so humble in the eyes of people, so much so that if he asks for permission to be with the elite, he is not permitted, and if he intercedes for someone, his intercession is not accepted.' (Bukhārī)

COMMENTARY

This hadith is a follow-up to the previous one and paints a picture of two contrasting people: the first one is the slave of money, fame, self-image, and prestige. The second one is a selfless person who—in the context of the hadith—joins an army to fight for a noble cause in the path of God. He does not care which position he is chosen to serve in, at the front or in the rear, and does not mind whether he gets any exposure or praise. The hadith is beautifully phrased in a form of supplication that praises the sincere servant of Allah and rebukes the servant of the materialistic life.

To put things in perspective, a Muslim who works for the sake of Allah is *not* in need of the spotlight, because he *or* she aims for excellence (*iḥsān*) in deeds, as defined in the famous hadith of Jibrīl: 'To worship Allah as though you see Him, for if you cannot see Him, then know that He sees you.' (Bukhārī and Muslim)

When we aim for *iḥsān* in activism and worship, we will always feel complete and satisfied. We should be assured that we worship a Master who sees all situations and intentions. We will have our hearts filled with Allah's recognition and attention. Whatever people observe or admire in us after that is just the surplus that flows from a heart that is filled with Allah's love.

Why is this essential to an activist's spirituality? Community work has a lot of glamorous aspects that usually accompany it: the mass following on social media, the big stage in major events, and receiving praise. All these factors may have an impact on one's sincerity and reduce or eliminate the spiritual benefits and blessings of what is supposed to be a major act of worship. Every Muslim activist shall be warned about seeking fame and material wealth, as in the hadith:

> *Ka'b ibn Mālik, may Allah be pleased with him, reported that the Messenger of Allah, may Allah bless him and give him peace, said: 'Two hungry wolves sent in the midst of a flock of sheep are no more destructive to them than a man's greed for wealth and fame is to his way of life or religion* (dīn).*'* (Tirmidhī)

A famous incident in Islamic history highlights this great quality of selflessness in the earlier generation of the Companions.[3] Before the battle of Yarmuk, which was a pivotal historical moment when the Muslims faced the Byzantine empire, Abū Bakr al-Ṣiddīq (RA) passed away and 'Umar ibn al-Khaṭṭāb (RA) took over the leadership as the caliph of the Muslims. Khālid ibn al-Walīd (RA), the legendary commander-in-chief, was leading the Muslim army and preparing for this critical battle. 'Umar (RA) was worried that Khālid's (RA) track record of victory and achievement might cause the Muslim community to become overly attached to his personality. This would result in them losing sight of the fact that victory only comes from Allah, which could have had detrimental implications for their faith. So 'Umar (RA) sent a message to Abū Ubaydah ibn al-Jarrāḥ (RA) to demote Khālid (RA) and take leadership in his place. When Abū 'Ubaydah (RA) received the letter, he hid it out of fear of causing dissension within the Muslim army, and only showed it to Khālid (RA) after the battle was over.

3 A.Y. Akrum, *Sayfullah Khalid ibn Al-Walid*, (Mu'ssaat Al-Risalah Beirut, 2007).

This incident shows a high sense of wisdom and sincerity on Abū ʿUbaydah's (RA) part, as he kept away from any personal inclination or preference. On the other hand, the response from Khālid (RA) was also remarkable, who immediately complied with ʿUmar's (RA) instructions and assumed his responsibility as a soldier under Abū ʿUbaydah's (RA) leadership. He did not even choose to isolate himself or leave the army, and some narrations even mention his memorable response: 'I fight to please Allah, the Lord of ʿUmar, not for the sake of ʿUmar himself!'

SUGGESTED ACTION ITEMS

1. This hadith highlights the importance of maintaining deeds that are only known between yourself and Allah, especially for those serving the community in the public space. This could be through private acts of worship, such as extra prayers, hidden charity, or even serving the community in a less visible setting, for example, cleaning the bathrooms of your local mosque. Allah acknowledges both the public and the private sphere in our lives and encourages us to do both. In a sense, the righteous people in a community should not keep hiding their good deeds while the sinners expose them. However, it goes without saying that private charity should be the default and preferred case.

If you give charity openly, it is good, but if you keep it secret and give to the needy in private, that is better for you, and it will atone for some of your bad deeds: God is well aware of all that you do. (al-Baqarah 2: 271)

2. Share stories of sincerity and selflessness with your team, both from the Companions' time as well as stories from your local community. Try to highlight individuals who may not get enough of the spotlight, such as the mothers and sisters in your community, the teacher at the masjid's Islamic studies classes, and your masjid security guard. Each of these is a shepherd who is tending to their flock within their capacity (see hadith 9), and we need to highlight their sincerity and their service.

3. A good leader must be an excellent follower, and the best speakers are the ones who listen more than talk. Make sure that one's ambitions to serve the community and influence the people does not come in the way of one's own education and spiritual development.

HADITH 3
THE DESTRUCTION OF ONE'S DEEDS

قال رسول الله صلى الله عليه وسلم: ما أخاف على أمَّتي إلَّا ثلاثًا : شُحٌّ مُطاعٌ ، وهوًى مُتَّبعٌ ، وإمامُ ضلالٍ (رواه الطبراني والبزار و صححه الألباني)

It is narrated that the Messenger of Allah, may Allah bless him and give him peace, said: 'I fear nothing for my community except three things: when greed and stinginess predominate, when whims and desires are followed, and when a leader rules with misguidance.' (Ṭabarānī and al-Bazzār)[4]

COMMENTARY

According to the Qur'an, the purification of the heart is a major requirement for attaining success in the Hereafter:

> **The Day when no one will benefit from wealth or children; But only one who comes to Allah with a sound heart.** (al-Shuʿarā' 26: 88-89)

Activism and community organization need to be protected from all types of spiritual diseases. In this hadith, the Prophet, may Allah bless him and give him peace, warns against three examples.

4 This hadith has been deemed as weak by many scholars, but its message is supported by many other hadith and Qur'anic references.

A. Predominance of Greed

Every human heart may contain an element of greed and love of worldly possessions. However, it should become alarming to us when the craving for worldly matters (wealth, power, fame, etc.) starts to control one's actions. As the following verse shows, we need to be watchful and protect our hearts from being inundated with greed.

> **And whoever is protected from the stinginess of his soul—it is those who will be the successful ones.** (al-Taghābun 64: 16)

Stinginess is a disease of the heart that is deeply rooted in different forms of human insecurities, such as having a scarcity mindset. In a sense, it causes the believer to dismiss the fact that Allah is the true provider and the true giver. Clearly, stinginess may manifest itself in different forms that are not limited to wealth and money. One could show their greed in continuously wanting to be the centre of attention and popularity, and become dissatisfied with less visible forms of community work (despite the praiseworthy attitude of working behind the scenes as in hadith 2). People may become stingy even in giving praise and recognizing the good work of others, assuming that giving credit to others may diminish the recognition that they dearly wish for themselves. Such an attitude may result in centring all the work and the success around themselves and their achievements. Their obedience to their egos takes different forms and craves for more than just material possessions.

B. Following Whims and Desires

The Arabic word for whims and desires is *hawā*, which refers to the act of dropping down, falling, or tumbling. It has other meanings of love, affection, craving, lust, and pleasure.[5] The implication of these meanings is that following one's desires, abandoning Divine guidance, and making desire an end in itself results in disgrace and falling from the ranks of the righteous.

In activism and community work, following desires manifests itself in different forms, such as base or carnal desires, such as sexual temptation between the genders. However, many desires today could be packaged in an intellectual or rational manner as not having the capability to understand certain rulings at a particular time in one's life. This may cause some individuals to abandon the whole act of submission to Allah and His wisdom, which is the essence of Islam, or to advocate certain ideologies by referring to Islamic teachings, by selectively choosing what fits that paradigm. Regarding such people, the Qur'an warns against taking whims and desires as one's source of legislation (and, eventually, as their god):

> **Have you seen the one who takes as his god his own desire? Are you to be his guardian?** (al-Furqān 25: 43)

Clearly, one cannot completely eradicate the personal desires and ambition in people's hearts and minds. Even the best generation of this community (*ummah*), the Prophet

5 Abdur Rashid Siddiqui, *Qur'ānic Keywords: A Reference Guide*, p. 79, (The Islamic Foundation 2015).

Muhammad's Companions, had those amongst them who looked for worldly gains:

> **Among you are some who desire this world, and among you are some who desire the Hereafter.** (āl ʿImran 3: 152)

What we really need is to always keep our desires in check, and never go around in life neglecting their presence and their potentially damaging effects. Allah Mighty and Majestic commanded the Messenger's wives, may Allah be pleased with them, to avoid speaking softly with other men to avoid instigating temptations in someone else's heart:

> **O wives of the Prophet, you are not like anyone among women. If you fear Allah, then do not be soft in speech [to men], lest he in whose heart is disease should covet, but speak with appropriate speech.** (al-Aḥzāb 33: 32)

C. Misguided leaders

One can think of the third segment of this hadith as the culmination of the first two. After all, political leaders, celebrities, and public figures with massive followings reflect the masses who either choose them or allow them to remain in power. So, this hadith warns against a moral crisis, represented by greed and following whims and desires that have reached all levels of a society, and that affect both spiritual and political leaders. It shows how the moral disaster of being led by greed and desire manifests itself with the emergence of corrupt leaders. Such leaders, in turn, themselves become role models for a life of mischief and sin, serving only to reinforce a vicious cycle of wrongdoing. This is why Islam teaches us that the Muslim community should resist misguided leaders from enforcing their ideologies and lifestyles on the masses. As an example, Allah narrates the story of a pharaoh who led his nation to destruction. Allah also specifically mentions how their behaviour and attitude made them partly to blame:

> **So he fooled his people, and they obeyed him. Indeed, they were [themselves] a people defiantly disobedient [of Allah].** (al-Zukhruf 43: 54)

SUGGESTED ACTION ITEMS

1. Ensure that transparency exists in your community in order to hold its leadership accountable for their actions and decisions. This can be done with the utmost respect and consideration, with a reminder that the ultimate goal is to help all members by protecting them from their egos and their moments of weakness. Clearly, building such environment requires time and effort, and may cause clashes and conflicts, especially in the presence of incompetent board members. While there are no easy solutions or quick fixes, a much-needed first step is to motivate the public to care enough about creating

the required checks and balances.[6] Without social pressure from the critical mass of the community—through donations, elections, or any other means—these leaders will not feel the need to challenge the status quo, because no one is really demanding such change. hadith 10 and 11 warn against reaching such levels of apathy within a community, as there is little hope for them to move out of it and induce real change.

2. Remind yourself and your team that leaders are human beings. They are prone to err and commit mistakes. We often tend to one of two absolutes when describing the situation of our leadership: we assume that our leaders should be as righteous as ʿUmar ibn al-Khaṭṭab (RA) or as evil as Abū Jahl. We need to realize that a human being can be at any level in between the two absolutes, with all the good and the bad that a human soul can carry.

3. It is understandable that male and female Muslim volunteers may need to interact within a team to organize and plan events. This ensures the best results for the group and limits the possibility of miscommunication and misalignment. However, it is important to stay within the boundaries of Islamic

6 Omar Usman, '5 Ways the Gas Station Owner Mentality Is Killing Our Masjids', *Muslim Matters*, 21 August 2017, https://muslimmatters.org/2017/08/21/5-ways-the-gas-station-owner-mentality-is-killing-our-masjids/. Accessed December 2019.

modesty and chastity, and limit the side-effects that may result from undisciplined interactions between the two genders—which may apply to young and single students as well as adults. Hence, it is important that the group initially establishes clear guidelines for the frequency, context and etiquette of such interactions, and limit these to avoid unwanted feelings and emotions from harming the members and the group's work.

HADITH 4
MERCY TO MANKIND

عَنِ ابْنِ عُمَرَ أَنَّ النَّبِيَّ صَلَّى اللَّهُ عَلَيْهِ وَسَلَّمَ قَال أَحَبُّ النَّاسِ إِلَى اللَّهِ أَنْفَعُهُمْ لِلنَّاسِ وَأَحَبُّ الأَعْمَالِ إِلَى اللَّهِ سُرُورٌ تُدْخِلُهُ عَلَى مُسْلِمٍ أَوْ تَكْشِفُ عَنْهُ كُرْبَةً أَوْ تَقْضِي عَنْهُ دِينًا أَوْ تَطْرُدُ عَنْهُ جُوعًا وَلَأَنْ أَمْشِيَ مَعَ أَخِيهِ فِي حَاجَةٍ أَحَبُّ إِلَيَّ مِنْ أَنْ أَعْتَكِفَ فِي هَذَا الْمَسْجِدِ شَهْرًا وَمَنْ كَفَّ غَضَبَهُ سَتَرَ اللَّهُ عَوْرَتَهُ وَمَنْ كَظَمَ غَيْظَهُ وَلَوْ شَاءَ أَنْ يُمْضِيَهُ أَمْضَاهُ مَلأَ اللَّهُ عَزَّ وَجَلَّ قَلْبَهُ أَمْنًا يَوْمَ الْقِيَامَةِ وَمَنْ مَشَى مَعَ أَخِيهِ فِي حَاجَةٍ حَتَّى أَثْبَتَهَا لَهُ أَثْبَتَ اللَّهُ عَزَّ وَجَلَّ قَدَمَهُ عَلَى الصِّرَاطِ يَوْمَ تَزِلُّ فِيهِ الأَقْدَامُ (الطبراني و صححه الألباني)

The most beloved people to Allah are those who are most beneficial to people. The most beloved deed to Allah is to make a Muslim happy, or to remove one of his troubles, or to forgive his debt, or to relieve his hunger. That I walk with a brother regarding a need is more beloved to me than that I seclude myself in this mosque in Madinah for a month. Whoever swallows his anger, then Allah will conceal his faults. Whoever suppresses his rage, even though he could fulfil his anger if he wished, then Allah will secure his heart on the Day of Resurrection. Whoever walks with his brother regarding a need until he secures it for him, then Allah Almighty will make his footing firm across the Bridge on the day when the footholds are shaken. (Ṭabarānī)

COMMENTARY

This hadith provides a grassroot definition of activism and spirituality, one that goes beyond the intellectual and academic discussions that take place at conventions and in lecture halls. Yes, you may have grandiose goals to change the world, but such plans should probably start with being a source of benefit and happiness to Allah's creations, rather than overlooking them.

Why is this hadith so important for Muslim activists? We should realize that people cannot fully comprehend the goals and objectives of a given cause if they are busy with putting food on the table and making ends meet. The hadith at hand invites community leaders and activists to address specific forms of distress that one may encounter such as debt and hunger, both being huge burdens on individuals, communities, and nations. The Prophet Muhammad, may Allah bless him and give him peace, used to seek refuge from both of them:

Abū Hurayrah (RA), reported that the Prophet, may Allah bless him and give him peace, used to say, 'O Allah, I seek refuge in You from hunger, for it is an evil bed-fellow, and I seek refuge in You from treachery, for it is an evil hidden trait.' (Abū Dāwūd)

Hadith 4 describes inner aspects of activism (our belief system) in addition to its outer aspects (our activities, deeds, and manners). The very first words of the hadith: 'the most beloved deeds to Allah' sets the tone for what follows, and places the right intention at the centre of any activism or service discussion (as in hadith 1 and 2). Moreover, the hadith confirms that not all deeds are equal in the eyes of Allah, and some have a higher priority than others. Activists should do their best to remove any bias and keep asking themselves: which act is more beloved to Allah at this moment in time, for this situation, for me or my group? We move on with the hadith to note the continued reference to the Day of Judgement, and the emphasis that a believer needs such good deeds on the Day of Judgement, more than the people he/she happens to serve. Moreover, the hadith mentions small deeds in singular form, such as feeding one person's hunger or paying off his debt, and motivates us to get started on that path, regardless of how small we may perceive a deed. For some people, suppressing one's internal anger (referred to as *ghayẓ*) or external anger (referred to as *ghaḍab*) could be the best form of charity and service. The hadith concludes with what can be considered as a warning to the believers: that bad manners may nullify the blessings and the impact of noble good deeds. Our service to the community is nothing but an element of our spiritual education and development (*tarbiyah* and *tazkiyah*). It should soften our hearts, improve our manners, and improve our self-awareness. This hadith should inspire activists and organizations to attain spirituality through service by focusing on the human element of the people you help.

SUGGESTED ACTION ITEMS

1. Resist the tendency to turn their suffering into just another number or statistic that is shared in the news. The hadith shares specific examples of being actively involved with helping, not just through financial donation, such as walking with a brother until you fulfil his need, even if this caused you to leave your preferred act of worship in the masjid. This may seem difficult, if not impossible, in an ever-complicated world with widespread disasters and challenges. However, the Qur'an indicates how attaining the spiritual development of the giver is in fact one of the objectives of charity:

   In order to cleanse and purify them [Prophet], accept a gift out of their property [to make amends] and pray for them—your prayer will be a comfort to them. (al-Tawbah 9:103)

2. Some suggested steps that can help us reclaim our spirituality in service, beyond financial support include: (i) trying to help fewer families, even one family, while having empathy with their situation, getting to know them more closely, and helping them to transform their life; (ii) build empathy with the needy by engaging in multiple acts of service—such as volunteer your time, pray for the people you help, cook food for them, teach their children; (iii) focus on community service efforts in your local community; (iv) be careful from the spiritual

ramifications that result from sharing pictures of community service work with a wider audience—such publicity puts one's sincerity in a high risk of becoming showing off, but it also dehumanizes the people that are being served, and turns them into marketing material to collect more funds.

3. An often overlooked form of charity that is mentioned in this hadith is to help those who are in debt. Sometimes we can judge debtors harshly, assuming that their indebtedness is their fault and so they are undeserving of our charity. However, the Qur'an mentions clearly that debt is one of the eight valid categories of *zakāt* (*al-Tawbah* 9: 60). We should revive this Sunnah and make sure that our charity does not follow our personal preferences, but rather fulfils all that pleases Allah. In addition, we need to direct our civic engagement towards resisting the corruption in policies as well as the financial institutions that feed off usury (*ribā*).

4. Reflect on the story of Prophet Yusuf, peace be upon him, and how he saved Egypt from poverty and starvation. Despite living under an oppressive and corrupt regime, he seized the opportunity to serve his community and its surrounding tribes without asking for any political gains that would serve his duties as a Prophet of Allah. It is well known that preaching the message of *tawḥīd* is an essential duty to all prophets; however, some activists may

mix social and charity work and *da'wah* work, which may result in both segments of their work to come off as inauthentic and opportunistic. We see in the example of Prophet Yūsuf how the Qur'an highlighted both his *da'wah* efforts, while imprisoned he invited his two companions (*Yūsuf* 12: 36-41) as well as his humanitarian and political dimension (*Yūsuf* 12: 55-57).

HADITH 5
COURAGE THROUGH DEEP CONNECTION WITH ALLAH

عن ابن عباس رضي الله عنهما قال: ' كنت خلف النبي ﷺ يوماً فقال: ' يا غلام إني أعلمك كلمات:' احفظ الله يحفظك، احفظ الله تجده تجاهك، إذا سألت فاسأل الله ، وإذا استعنت فاستعن بالله، واعلم: أن الأمة لو اجتمعت على أن ينفعوك بشيء، لم ينفعوك إلا بشيء قد كتبه الله لك، وإن اجتمعوا على أن يضروك بشيء، لم يضروك بشيء إلا بشيء قد كتبه الله عليك؛ رفعت الأقلام، وجفت الصحف' (الترمذي و أحمد و الحاكم).

Ibn 'Abbās reported: I was riding behind the Messenger of Allah, may Allah bless him and give him peace, when he said to me, 'Young man, I will teach you some words. Be mindful of Allah and He will protect you. Be mindful of Allah and you will find Him before you. If you ask, ask from Allah. If you seek help, seek help from Allah. Know that if all the nations gathered together to benefit you, they could not benefit you unless Allah has decreed it for you. And if all the nations gathered together to harm you, they could not harm you unless Allah has decreed it for you. The pens have been lifted and [the ink on] the pages [has] dried.' (Tirmidhī, Aḥmad and al-Ḥākim)

COMMENTARY

Activists and reformers—by the very nature of their mission—are expected to go against the flow and challenge the status quo. By doing so, they put their families, livelihood, careers, and sometimes their own safety at stake. Hence, they need a strong and deep connection with Allah and a strong conviction that nothing will befall upon them outside of His will or permission. They need frequent reminders of statements such as the one attributed to 'Alī ibn Abī Ṭālib, may Allah be pleased with him: 'By Allah, I don't care whether death falls on me or I fall on it!'

Yes, we need the motivation and support from people around us. We need the right combination of mentors, supporters, and followers. But, at the end of the day, we must affirm that, first and foremost, our support comes from Allah alone.

Prophet Mūsā, may Allah send him peace, witnessed fear in multiple moments of his life:

> **And he became inside the city fearful and anticipating exposure.** (al-Qaṣaṣ 28:18)

> **So he left it, fearful and anticipating [apprehension].** (al-Qaṣaṣ 28:21)

Allah said, 'Seize it and fear not; We will return it to its former condition.' (Ṭa Ha 20:21)

In almost all the moments of fear he experienced in his life, Musa was connected to Allah. He could have never handled it by himself, and he realized that he needed to seek help and strength from Allah. The Prophet Mūsā's connection with Allah kept getting stronger and stronger, until the day he led the Israelites out of Egypt with Pharaoh and his army following them. At this most challenging moment in his life, with the sea in front of him and his enemies behind him, his connection with Allah was also at its highest:

And when the two companies saw one another, the companions of Musa said, 'Indeed, we are to be overtaken!' [Mūsā] said, 'No! Indeed, with me is my Lord; He will guide me.' (al-Shuʿarā' 26:61-62)

ACTION ITEMS FROM THIS BEAUTIFUL HADITH

1. This hadith encourages us to have an attitude of risk-taking, to seek out new experiences and get outside of our comfort zone. Muslims should overcome the fear of poverty or low social status, which is unfortunately driving most of our career and life choices. A clear example is when our community disproportionately emphasize certain fields of study, such as medicine, engineering, law, for example., regardless of whether the student has

the right skills and passion for such a field. Yes, it is important to tie one's camel and be mindful about worldly materialistic means. However, the belief in the names of Allah as the Provider (*Al-Razzāq*), the Protector (*Al-Wakil*), and the True Giver (*Al-Wahhāb*) should be present as well. Such belief should be reflected in the spirit of sacrifice and risk-taking, which is deeply rooted in our Islamic principles and worldview.

2. Muslims should resort to the following saying: Allah is sufficient for us, and He is the best of Guardians (*dhikr: ḥasbunā'Llāhu wa ni'ma'l-wakīl*), especially when being targeted because of their faith. This was the supplication (*du'ā'*) that most prophets used when they experienced fear:

   Those whose faith only increased when people said, 'Fear your enemy: they have amassed a great army against you,' and who replied, 'God is enough for us: He is the best protector.' (āl 'Imrān 3: 173)

3. Our educational programmes and lectures should instil in our community the values of sacrifice, trust in Allah, and patience, especially in times of trial and tribulation. The early Companions went through a lot of turmoil and persecution, and the Divine guidance of the Makkan period emphasize these themes. The Companions themselves—despite being very strong in their faith—had moments of weakness

where they expressed their fears to the Messenger, may Allah bless him and give him peace. The story of Khabbāb (RA) reveals these complaints and the Prophet's response to them. The Companion Khabbāb ibn al-Aratt (RA) narrates that:

We complained to Allah's Messenger, may Allah bless him and give him peace, of the persecution inflicted on us by the disbelievers while he was sitting in the shade of the Kaaba, leaning on his garment. We asked him, 'Would you seek help for us? Would you pray to Allah for us?' He replied, 'Among the nations before you, a believer would be put in a hole that was dug for him, a saw would be put on his head, and he would be cut into two pieces—yet that torture would not make him give up his religion. His body would be scored with iron combs that would remove the flesh from his bones and nerves, yet that would not make him abandon his religion. By Allah, this religion of Islam will prevail till a traveller from Sana'a [in Yemen] to Hadramawt will fear none but Allah, or a wolf as regards his sheep, but you [people] are hasty.' (Bukhārī)

4. This hadith shows the great attention that the Messenger of Allah, may Allah bless him and give him peace, gave the young Companions, and how he instilled faith in their hearts at an early age. It shows how he (i) spent quality time with Ibn 'Abbās (RA); (ii) waited for the right teaching moment; (iii) used easy and understandable language; and (iv) made sure Ibn 'Abbās (RA) prioritized his relationship with Allah first, (v) and lowered his sense of reliance upon people.

HADITH 6
THE ROAD LESS TRAVELLED

عَنْ أَبِي هُرَيْرَةَ، قَالَ: قَالَ رَسُولُ اللَّهِ صلى الله عليه وسلم ' سَيَأْتِي عَلَى النَّاسِ سَنَوَاتٌ خَدَّاعَاتٌ يُصَدَّقُ فِيهَا الْكَاذِبُ وَيُكَذَّبُ فِيهَا الصَّادِقُ وَيُؤْتَمَنُ فِيهَا الْخَائِنُ وَيُخَوَّنُ فِيهَا الأَمِينُ وَيَنْطِقُ فِيهَا الرُّوَيْبِضَةُ قِيلَ وَمَا الرُّوَيْبِضَةُ قَالَ الرَّجُلُ التَّافِهُ فِي أَمْرِ الْعَامَّةِ ' . (إبن ماجة و أحمد و الحاكم)

Abū Huraryah (RA) narrated that the Messenger of Allah, may Allah bless him and give him peace, said, 'Years of treachery will come to the people when the liar will be regarded as honest and the honest person will be treated as a liar. The traitor will be regarded as faithful, and the faithful person will be seen as a traitor, and the ruwaybiḍah *will speak out about public affairs.' It was asked, 'Who are the* ruwaybiḍah*?' He said: 'Vile and petty men who speak out about the affairs of the masses.'* (Ibn Mājah, Aḥmad, and al-Ḥākim)

COMMENTARY

This hadith prophesizes the trials and tribulations that will befall upon humanity as the world gets closer to the Day of Judgement. It addresses the erosion of objective values of truth and integrity, especially in public life. One may understand from the language of this hadith that it is referring to corrupt political leaders, shallow pundits and media figures, and any public figure who may directly and negatively influence policies, economies, and people's livelihoods due to reckless and ill-informed decisions. Moreover, this hadith may also include celebrities in the entertainment industry who promote a lifestyle of sin and heedlessness, who rely on people becoming obsessed with their opinion on everything that they eat, dress, or buy. Finally, the *ruwaybiḍah* may also refer to those who speak on behalf of Islam without knowledge, even if given scholarly status and titles. The presence of such individuals and discourses can become extremely problematic, especially when accompanied by the scarcity of the real scholars, as explained in this hadith:

> *'Abdullāh ibn 'Amr ibn al-'Āṣ (RA), reported that, 'I heard the Messenger of Allah, may Allah bless him and give him peace, saying, 'Verily, Allah does not take away knowledge by snatching it from the people, but He removes it by taking away [the lives of] the religious scholars till none of the scholars remain. Then the people will take ignorant ones as their leaders, who, when asked to deliver religious verdicts, will issue them without knowledge, the result being that they will go astray and will lead others astray'.* (Bukhārī and Muslim)

HOW CAN WE PROTECT OURSELVES AND OUR COMMUNITY FROM THE *RUWAYBIḌAH* EFFECT?

1. Allah has warned us on multiple occasions about conforming heedlessly to the herd mentality, so we are not impressed simply with following the majority and wherever they may lead us:

And if you obey most of those upon the earth, they will mislead you from the way of Allah. They follow idle fancies, indulging in conjecture. (al-An'ām 6: 116)

In addition, the Messenger, may Allah bless him and give him peace, gave glad tidings to those who felt they are strangers due to their commitment to Islam:

Abū Hurayrah (RA) narrated that the Messenger of Allah, may Allah bless him and give him peace, said: Islam started as something strange, and it will revert to being strange again, so give glad tidings to the strangers. (Muslim)

This hadith tells us that the Muslim values of truth, justice and chastity may never become popular and mainstream. This should never surprise us, persuade us from our religion or cause us to shy away from speaking the truth and holding on to an unpopular opinion (as in hadith 13). However, this should not result in the Muslim community members excluding others from our circles, as taught by hadith 21, 32, and 35.

2. In our assessment of our activities and events, we should put less emphasis on the turnout and the size of our attendance and focus on how effective our message was in inspiring, educating, and transforming our audience or some of its members.

While marketing and public relations are essential elements of any programme, they should not become the main drivers of our decision making. Our values should not be twisted or tweaked for the sake of appealing to more people at any cost. We should also bear in mind that some prophets will come on the Day of Judgement with very few believers from their nation, because truth is not defined simply by following the majority, as the Prophet, may Allah bless him and give him peace, said:

'Some nations were displayed before me. A prophet would pass in front of me with one man, and another with two men, and another with a group of people. and another with nobody with him.' (Bukhārī)

3. This hadith warns us not to be deluded by the amount of media attention or fame that any influential figure may have. Ultimately, such person is a human being with all the weaknesses and inclinations that any human has. Moreover, the believers are instructed not to blindly follow anyone, without referring his or her motives or actions to the Qur'an and the Sunnah, as in the saying that is attributed to 'Alī ibn Abī Ṭālib (RA), may Allah be pleased with him:

   'Truth cannot be identified by following men! Follow the truth and you shall identify its people.'

CHAPTER 2

THE WHAT [1]

COMMUNITY SERVICE: THE SOCIAL RESPONSIBILITY OF MUSLIM ACTIVISTS

A MUSLIM ACTIVIST cannot lead people, whether in *da'wah*, teaching, politics, or any other field, without demonstrating love and care for them through service. The Messenger of Allah, may Allah bless him and give him peace, spent forty years before prophethood in Makkah, and those years helped build his credibility amongst his own people: as the honest and the trustworthy merchant, and as the charitable man who never turned down any request for help, and as the connected community member who always stood by the weak and the needy. His credibility was manifested in their reply to him after he stood on the mountain of Ṣafā to announce publicly the message of Islam to the Quraysh and said:

> *'If I were to tell you that an army with horsemen were advancing to attack you from the valley on the other side of this hill, would you believe me?', and the people said: 'yes, we have never seen you lie before this day'. And he replied: 'I am here to warn you before a severe punishment reaches you.'* (Bukhārī)

Chapter 2 builds on the definition of activism given in the introduction of this book and connects the dots between the themes of Chapter 1 (spirituality) and Chapter 3 (political activism). The immediate outcome of having a sincere relationship with our Creator is to serve His creation. Such service in turn becomes a cornerstone in a community's political activism, by fulfilling the duty of enjoining good and forbidding evil.

HADITH 7
WINNING THE HEARTS

عَنْ عَبْدِ اللَّهِ بْنِ سَلاَمٍ، قَالَ لَمَّا قَدِمَ رَسُولُ اللَّهِ ﷺ الْمَدِينَةَ انْجَفَلَ النَّاسُ إِلَيْهِ وَقِيلَ قَدِمَ رَسُولُ اللَّهِ ﷺ قَدِمَ رَسُولُ اللَّهِ ﷺ قَدِمَ رَسُولُ اللَّهِ ﷺ فَجِئْتُ فِي النَّاسِ لأَنْظُرَ إِلَيْهِ فَلَمَّا اسْتَبَنْتُ وَجْهَ رَسُولِ اللَّهِ ﷺ عَرَفْتُ أَنَّ وَجْهَهُ لَيْسَ بِوَجْهِ كَذَّابٍ وَكَانَ أَوَّلَ شَيْءٍ تَكَلَّمَ بِهِ أَنْ قَالَ ' أَيُّهَا النَّاسُ أَفْشُوا السَّلاَمَ وَأَطْعِمُوا الطَّعَامَ وَصَلُّوا وَالنَّاسُ نِيَامٌ تَدْخُلُونَ الْجَنَّةَ بِسَلاَمٍ ' . (الترمذي)

When the Prophet, may Allah bless him and give him peace, arrived in Madinah, people came out to meet him. It was said that the Messenger of Allah, may Allah bless him and give him peace, had arrived, so I went among the people to get a look at him. When I gazed upon the face of the Messenger of Allah, may Allah bless him and give him peace, I knew that this face was not the face of a liar. The first thing that I heard him speak was: 'O you people! Spread peace, feed others, and pray in the night while people are sleeping: you will enter Paradise with the greeting of peace.' (Tirmidhī)

COMMENTARY

In the early days of Madinah, after the migration of Prophet Muhammad, may Allah bless him and give him peace, the Muslims lived as a minority amongst multiple other communities within a complicated tribal system: two Arab tribes (al-Aws and al-Khazraj) in addition to multiple Jewish ones (Banū Al-Naḍīr, Banū Qaynuqā', and Banū Qurayẓah). On the political side, the Arabs were recovering from a civil war that depleted their resources and took away multiple lives. On the religious side, some of the Arabs converted to Islam while others remained withholding their pagan faith. Throughout history, migration and attempts to blend communities of multiple origins were often accompanied by hatred, divisiveness, and even bloodshed. However, in the migration to Madinah, we see a deliberate approach from Prophet Muhammad, may Allah bless him and give him peace, to mitigate these divisions. This was manifested in his first speech after the migration when he laid down the first steps towards breaking the barriers between different community segments. This marvellous prophetic speech served the immediate needs of the community and merged activism, social work, and spiritual enlightenment in a recipe that can only come from a Prophet:

Spread peace! Fight fear mongering and divisive tendencies. Greet others with 'As-salāmu 'alaykum' and break the ice to establish that human connection. Especially after years of civil war and bloodshed, the message of 'Islam bringing peace to Madinah' should be reinforced and practiced by the speeches and actions of the Muslim leadership as well as by the public.

Feed the people! The new migration should not result in a noticeable economic loss to the indigenous population, and no hungry person should be left out! Also, sharing meals with strangers cannot but bring the hearts together and encourage intimate social interaction. The Prophet, may Allah bless him and give him peace, instilled a service mindset in the Companions which is a necessary prerequisite for any *da'wah* or grassroot activism.

Connect with your family (according to some narrations): Even if those family members are not Muslim, or if there are previous injustices, such as war, that make it awkward to initiate that connection. Commands like this helped solidify the cohesion among communities, contrary to the claim that Islam resulted in cutting off family ties.

Pray at night! This part represents the essence of Islamic activism: combining community work (feeding people, spreading peace) with spirituality and worship (praying at night). Muslims should strive for a sincere and private relationship with their Lord, and nurture their souls in parallel to all the public service and activities that they engage in. This calls upon the essential element of Divine help and blessing (*barakah*) needed for the activism and seeks acceptance from Allah first and then from the people.

As a reward to all of this, the Prophet, may Allah bless him and give him peace, promised Paradise to those who maintain this balance between public and private life, and serve their people while humbling themselves to Allah. The guarantee of peace does not only include the final destination (Paradise) but also the journey to get there in peace and tranquillity, if Allah wills, as the hadith ends with saying that you enter Jannah with peace.

It is also fascinating that this hadith addresses multiple circles of influence that Muslims should engage with:

Circle 1: The whole community. Even those who may not know you or come to your events should feel safe and secure in your presence and from your contributions. The action item with them is to spread peace.

Circle 2: Individuals with whom you deal regularly, as well as the poor, the needy, and the destitute. For this audience, you may give them a direct invitation for dinner, or simply invite them over for lunch! The action item is to feed the people.

Circle 3: Your immediate family members. Do not surrender to the Western liberal notion of abandoning family ties while pursuing your self-interest! The action item is to make that call and reconnect severed relationships.

Circle 4: One can see how the circles of influence shrink from the public to the inner and private: the last one is your own self and within your own heart. Pray at night and develop and maintain a sincere connection with Allah, glorified and exalted is He.

ACTION ITEMS

1. Muslim public speakers and educators should ensure that their education and message fit the needs of the community and addresses their issues. The Prophet, may Allah bless him and give him peace, in this hadith gave the Companions a roadmap to the most needed actionable items that (i) cemented the community together and (ii) were easily implemented by everyone. A *khuṭbah* that is disconnected from people's concerns and does not motivate them towards clear actions may cause the community to give up on allowing Islam to enter their lives and guide their actions.

2. The Messenger, may Allah bless him and give him peace, encouraged the Companions to pray their extra Sunnah prayers at home and not in the masjid. Simply put, the message is to ensure that the spirituality that you gain from your community interactions penetrates your lifestyle and your choices inside your own home. Abū Hurayrah, may Allah be pleased with him, reported:

I heard the Messenger of Allah, may Allah bless him and give him peace, saying, 'Do not turn your houses into graveyards. Satan runs away from the house in which Surah al-Baqarah *is recited.'* (Muslim)

3. Don't feel afraid or shy to share spiritual enlightenment even with non-Muslims. Many people are searching for the mix and holistic approach to the mind-body-soul that Islam offers. It is interesting that this hadith was narrated by 'Abdullāh ibn Salām, a Jewish scholar who attended the sermon to learn more about the Messenger, may Allah bless him and give him peace, and eventually accepted Islam. There may be many 'Abdullāhs' around you who might follow a similar path.

4. This hadith encourages us to revive the Sunnah of serving food to our audience and attendees in Muslim events and be intentional about it. In addition to lectures and workshops, sharing our cultural food and sweets may serve as a much-needed ice breaker that helps in building bonds between different factions of the community.

HADITH 8
FAITH, MANNERS, AND ACTION

عن النبي ﷺ قال: ' الإيمان بضع وسبعون، أو بضع وستون شعبة: فأفضلها قول لا إله إلا الله، وأدناها إماطة الأذى عن الطريق، والحياء شعبة من الإيمان' (متفق عليه).

The Prophet, may Allah bless him and give him peace, said: 'Īmān *has over 70 branches—or over 60 branches—the uppermost of which is to declare the testimony of faith, 'None has the right to be worshipped but Allah'; and the least of which is the removal of a harmful object from the road, and modesty is a branch of* īmān.' (Bukhārī and Muslim)

COMMENTARY

Islam's definition of righteousness encompasses all elements of a believer's existence. Starting from a sound belief in Allah, it trickles down to our character, and eventually to how we deal with all of God's creations. Without such understanding, our implementation of the faith will always be imbalanced. While the Messenger, may Allah bless him and give him peace, did not specify all 70 branches,[7] he provided three examples to manifest the holistic and encompassing nature of Islam:

Belief, represented by declaring the testimony of faith: According to Islamic principles, associating partners with Allah (*shirk*) is the root of all evil, and affirming monotheism

7 Many scholars attempted to compile those branches, such as *al-Bayhaqī* (*Shu'ab al-Īmān*) and Abū 'Abdullāh al-Ḥalīmī *(al-Minhāj)*.

(*tawḥīd*) is key for all acts of righteousness. For every deed to be deemed acceptable in Islam, it has to be performed with the intention to please Allah—centred around there being no deity worthy of worship except Allah (*lā ilāha illā Allāh*) and according to the path of His Prophet—following Muhammad as the Messenger of Allah (*Muḥammadun Rasūlu Allah*).

Without a *tawḥīd*-based frame of reference, activists are left to their whims and desires (as in hadith 3) to determine *what* to focus on and *how* to direct their political and social activism. A Muslim who understands *lā ilāha illā Allāh* should firmly believe that no real and comprehensive solution to humanity's problems exists except through what Allah demands and wants: This is true for a community—political and economic reform, fighting racism, for example—as much as for individuals, such as mental and spiritual wellbeing, family relations.

Manners, having a sense of modesty, bashfulness, and shame (*ḥayā'*): Linguistically, *haya'* is derived from the same root word as *ḥayāt* (life), indicating, as Ibn al-Qayyim says, that the life of the heart is in its modesty. The Prophet Muhammad, may Allah bless him and give him peace, also said, as narrated by Imam Malik: *'Every religion has a central character, and the character of Islam is modesty.'*

Why is *ḥayā'* so important? Ibn al-Qayyim explains how having such a character restrains a person from undertaking blameworthy actions, speech and thoughts. It is an internal state of the heart that pushes the believer to always act in a dignified manner in public (*ḥayā'* from the people) and in private (*ḥayā'* from Allah). For those who serve the Muslim community, such manners should be reflected in the environments we establish for our events, such as modest dress code and lowering our gaze, among others. Prophet Muhammad, may Allah bless him and give him peace, said:

> *'Modesty does not bring anything but goodness.'* (Muslim)

Action (removing harm from the streets): This part of the hadith reminds us of our responsibility as vicegerents on Allah's earth. Often deemed insignificant, such deeds have deeper implications from an activist and community-building perspective. It rectifies the individualistic tendencies of some people that causes them to detach themselves from accountability and blame others. This is especially true when the responsibility is shared between multiple unknown people; 'After all,' they may say, 'this garbage on the road is not really *my* responsibility! I did not really cause it, and I may not be directly affected by it!'

Moreover, people may find it difficult to direct acts of kindness towards an abstract entity such as the *ummah*, the local community, or the environment. The same people may have a great deal of empathy towards a specific person, such as a blind person across the street. This is why the hadith places great emphasis on deeds that may go unnoticed, without the need for rewards and words of thanks and praise.

It is important to note that the word harm (*adhā*) in this hadith should not be limited to the most primitive forms of physical harm, such as random garbage or banana peels, for example. Rather, Muslim activists should investigate all sources of harm in people's ways, such as pollution of the environment, or reckless driving. The 'harm in people's way' may include shameless ads, billboards, shows, and public material that affect people's modesty and promote a life of sin. This hadith realizes the holistic objectives of the Islamic Shariah, which aim at protecting people's faith (through *tawḥīd*), manners (through *ḥayā'*), and safety (through removing harm from the streets).

ACTION ITEMS AND FURTHER DISCUSSION

1. Muslim activists should understand the connection between faith, manners and social justice, and eventually step up to fulfil their responsibility in communicating a prophetic solution to humanity's problems through *tawḥīd*. Malcolm-X, understood that profound link in the context of social justice when he wrote:

   If white Americans could accept the religion of Islam, if they could accept the Oneness of God (Allah) they too could then sincerely accept the Oneness of Men, and cease to measure others always in terms of their 'difference in color'. And with racism now plaguing America like an incurable cancer, all thinking Americans should be more respective to Islam as an already proven solution to the race problem.

2. Muslim activists should act locally in their neighbourhoods to revive the Sunnah of the 'right of the road' as explained in this hadith :

   Abū Sa'īd al-Khudrī (RA) narrated that the Messenger of Allah, may Allah bless him and give him peace, said: 'Avoid sitting by the roadside.' The people then said, 'O Allah's Messenger, we cannot do without those meeting places in which we converse.' So he said, 'Well, if you insist [on that] give the road its due rights.' They asked, 'What are the road's due rights?' He replied, 'Lowering your gaze, abstaining from anything offensive, returning salutations, enjoining right (ma'rūf) *and forbidding wrong* (munkar).*'* (Bukhārī and Muslim)

3. Recognize those who work behind the scenes and do tasks that may seem simple or less sophisticated than other public tasks. The story of the lady who used to clean the masjid should serve as a huge inspiration in this regard. The Prophet Muhammad, may Allah bless him and give him peace, recognized her efforts, and went out of his way to perform the funeral prayer (*janazah*) for her when she passed away. Our organizations should apply the Sunnah of recognizing the efforts that go unnoticed and encourage contributions from all community members.

4. It is sad and unfortunate to see some cultures in the Muslim world belittle certain behaviours, such

as respect for traffic rules in a masjid parking lot, standing in line, or even organizing our shoes, despite having a whole surah in the Qur'an named Surah *al-Ṣaff* (Solid Lines, Chapter 61), and having the following strong hadith warning against harming people and blocking their way:

Ḥudhayfah ibn Usayd narrated that the Messenger of Allah, may Allah bless him and give him peace, said, 'Whoever harms the Muslims in their local roads deserves to be cursed by them.' (Ṭabarānī)

HADITH 9
THE SHEPHERD AND THE FLOCK: RESPONSIBILITY AT ALL LEVELS

عَنْ عَبْدِ اللَّهِ بْنِ عُمَرَ رَضِيَ اللَّهُ عَنْهُمَا أَنَّ رَسُولَ اللَّهِ صَلَّى اللَّهُ عَلَيْهِ وَسَلَّمَ قَالَ أَلَا كُلُّكُمْ رَاعٍ وَكُلُّكُمْ مَسْئُولٌ عَنْ رَعِيَّتِهِ فَالْإِمَامُ الَّذِي عَلَى النَّاسِ رَاعٍ وَهُوَ مَسْئُولٌ عَنْ رَعِيَّتِهِ وَالرَّجُلُ رَاعٍ عَلَى أَهْلِ بَيْتِهِ وَهُوَ مَسْئُولٌ عَنْ رَعِيَّتِهِ وَالْمَرْأَةُ رَاعِيَةٌ عَلَى أَهْلِ بَيْتِ زَوْجِهَا وَوَلَدِهِ وَهِيَ مَسْئُولَةٌ عَنْهُمْ وَعَبْدُ الرَّجُلِ رَاعٍ عَلَى مَالِ سَيِّدِهِ وَهُوَ مَسْئُولٌ عَنْهُ أَلَا فَكُلُّكُمْ رَاعٍ وَكُلُّكُمْ مَسْئُولٌ عَنْ رَعِيَّتِهِ

Abdullah ibn Umar reported: The Messenger of Allah, peace and blessings be upon him, said: 'Every one of you is a shepherd and is responsible for his flock. The leader of people is a guardian and is responsible for his subjects. A man is the guardian of his family and he is responsible for them. A woman is the guardian of her husband's home and his children and she is responsible for them. The servant of a man is a guardian

> *of the property of his master and he is responsible for it. No doubt, every one of you is a shepherd and is responsible for his flock.'* (Bukhārī)

COMMENTARY

People often associate activism with the political arena and the public space, and this may cause the rest of the Muslim community to belittle their roles and feel left out. What about the professional people who are busy in making a living, mothers who are taking care of their babies, and the youth who do not have a say in public affairs? In this beautiful hadith, the Prophet, may Allah bless him and give him peace, emphasizes leadership at all levels, even when it comes to servants who are entrusted with the property of their masters. It all depends on understanding that our position and role in life is not disconnected from the act of service that is needed from us. In other words, you *are* already a shepherd, and you *do* have responsibility, so go ahead and start tending to your flock.

The Prophet Muhammad, may Allah bless him and give him peace, used the relevant analogy of a shepherd, which is key in understanding the leadership of all prophets. Abū Hurayrah narrates:

> *'The Messenger of Allah, may Allah bless him and give him peace, said, "Every prophet has tended sheep." He was asked: "And did you?" He replied, "Yes, I used to take care of them for some Makkan families in return for a few coins."'* (Bukhārī)

In such a role, the prophets were exposed to a rough life at an early stage. A shepherd constantly watches over his sheep. He protects them from internal threats, such as sheep hurting themselves, or external ones like wolves. A shepherd must find the right balance between tending to individual sheep while keeping in mind the major decisions that affect the flock.

In addition, this hadith tells every shepherd to take care of *his* or *her* respective flock first! This may have been obvious for the ancient Arabs not to be consumed by how others tended their herds. However, in our modern world, some of us may forget or ignore this important point. Muslim activists need to stay in their lane and understand their roles and responsibilities in the grand scheme of things. When someone is focusing on their own flock, their own family, or their own task and duties, they are less likely to criticize others and interfere with their flock. They will be truly minding their own business, and hence implementing excellence in their faith:

> *On the authority of Abū Hurayrah, may Allah be pleased with him, who said: The Messenger of Allah, may Allah bless him and give him peace, said, 'A part of the excellence in one's faith is his leaving that which does not concern him.'* (Tirmidhī)

ACTION ITEMS

1. This hadith can inspire a personal or a team reflection activity to understand our circle of concern–the causes that you care for–and our circle of influence[8]; the knobs that you can turn in order to bring noticeable change. Normally, the causes that we care about have a much wider scope than our ability to change them. However, the more time we spend on what we can really influence–our own family, our local community, and, of course, our selves–the more we can expand and strengthen our circle of influence. Such an exercise should help us identify the 'sheep' that we should tend to as 'shepherds'.

2. A believer should ensure that the most basic of responsibilities are being fulfilled (towards parents, siblings, spouses, and children) and prioritize them over other ones. Allah says:

   O you who have believed, protect yourselves and your families from a Fire whose fuel is people and stones. (al-Taḥrīm 66: 6)

   This is of particular importance to Muslim women who may feel stressed out and want to give more to the community in different capacities. While society can never function well without their contribution

8 Stephen Covey, *The Seven Habits of Highly Effective People* (Free Press, 1989).

outside of the home; the hadith emphasizes that a woman's greatest impact is in securing the emotional wellbeing of the whole family. This is the 'flock' that only women can be the right shepherds for, as only they can secure it and protect its emotional stability and wellbeing.

3. The hadith emphasizes the word *'mas'ūl'* which goes beyond being 'responsible' to indicate being questioned and held accountable; the mindset of being questioned on the Day of Judgement before Allah should govern our thoughts before any worldly considerations:

   And stop them; indeed, they are to be questioned (al-Ṣāffāt 37: 24).

4. This hadith, among many others, inspired leaders such as 'Umar ibn al-Khaṭṭāb (RA), who took this responsibility and questioning to heart, and in a famous statement he said: 'By Allah, if a donkey tripped in Iraq, then I am concerned that Allah will ask me: why didn't you pave the road for it, O 'Umar?'

HADITH 10
THE RIGHTEOUS ONE WHO DOES NOT CARE!

عن مَالِكٌ، أَنَّهُ بَلَغَهُ أَنَّ أُمَّ سَلَمَةَ، زَوْجَ النَّبِيِّ ﷺ قَالَتْ يَا رَسُولَ اللَّهِ أَنَهْلِكُ وَفِينَا
الصَّالِحُونَ فَقَالَ رَسُولُ اللَّهِ ﷺ ' نَعَمْ إِذَا كَثُرَ الْخَبَثُ ' . (مالك)

Malik narrates that he had heard Umm Salamah, the wife of the Prophet, may Allah bless him and give him peace, who said, 'O Messenger of Allah! Shall we be destroyed while there are righteous people among us?' The Messenger of Allah, may Allah bless him and give him peace, said, "Yes, if wickedness prevails."' (Mālik)

COMMENTARY

This hadith differentiates between two important keywords that describe a Muslim's commitment to Islamic teachings: a righteous (*ṣāliḥ*) person versus a reformer (*muṣliḥ*). A *ṣāliḥ* is a religious person who performs his or her individual duties, including five daily prayers, fasting, charity, among others. A *muṣliḥ* goes beyond that to protect a community from wrongdoing (by forbidding evil), while spreading good as much as possible (by enjoining good). To protect from communal punishment, the believers shall ensure that they have enough reformers among them:

> **And your Lord would not have destroyed the cities unjustly while their people were reformers.** (Hūd 11: 117)

By engaging in social and spiritual reform, Muslims will be first and foremost protecting their own *dīn* and their own spirituality. A righteous person who keeps his faith to himself will eventually come under the influence of others, no matter how much he tries to resist. Even one's personal *du'ā'* and spiritual connection with Allah may risk becoming unanswered when activism is ignored:

> *By the one in whose hand is my soul, you will enjoin good and forbid evil or else Allah will soon send the punishment upon you. Then you will supplicate to Allah and He will not accept it from you.* (Tirmidhī)

The message from this hadith, and all the supporting evidence, is that fulfilling the Divine duty of enjoining good and forbidding evil is not optional in Islam. Muslims are expected to stand up against all that's forbidden by Allah Almighty, whether it is oppression, racism, shameless acts, or lewd behaviour. Not only that, Muslims are not entitled to practise a toned-down version of activism, where they enjoin good but don't forbid evil. Sometimes in their attempt to appeal to a larger audience or to fit Islam to a modernist framework, activists may encourage good and positive behaviour in people, but shy away from difficult conversations that need to be addressed. This would not be very different from nurturing a community with the right food but without curing it of its diseases. The Qur'an warns against such behaviour that also appeared in communities and nations before us:

Those Children of Israel who defied [God] were rejected through the words of David, and Jesus, son of Mary, because they disobeyed, they persistently overstepped the limits, they did not forbid each other to do wrong. How vile their deeds were! (al-Mā'idah 5: 78-79)

SUGGESTED ACTION ITEMS BASED ON THIS HADITH

1. Write down a sincere message to a friend or a community member who can be described as a *ṣāliḥ* but not as a *muṣliḥ*, somone who is inclined to individual acts of worship but who does not engage in public service. Include some specific advice on why they should consider getting out of their comfort zone and volunteering for a collective cause.

2. Some sincere Muslims may assume they are not 'good enough' to advise others, as they do not practise Islam properly themselves. To stay away from hypocrisy, they may also shy away from any community involvement such as teaching others, giving advice, or assuming a leadership position and they may justify their position through this *ayah*:

   Do you enjoin righteousness upon people while you ignore your own selves? (al-Baqarah 2: 44)

The keyword here is that a person shall not ignore *reminding* themselves when they remind others. Al-Saʿdī comments on this *āyah*:

There is nothing in the verse to indicate that if a person does not practise what he preaches, then he should give up enjoining good and forbidding evil. It is well known that a Muslim has two duties: enjoining (good) and forbidding (evil) to others, and doing likewise for himself. The fact that he gives up doing one of them does not mean that he has a concession allowing him to give up the other. Perfection is attained when the individual does both duties, and the worst-case scenario is when he gives up both. As for doing one of them and not the other, it is not as good as the former, but it is not as bad as the latter. Moreover, it is human nature that people do not follow those whose deeds contradict their words; deeds are more likely to be heeded and emulated than mere words.[9]

3. Encourage your group to recite Surah *al-ʿAsr* (Chapter 103) at the end of each meeting. Remind them that even when discussing logistics and details of an event, these meetings should be an embodiment of this surah. In other words, our meetings shall embody some or all of the following: (i) belief, (ii) righteous deeds, (iii) encouraging each other towards truth, and (iv) encouraging each other towards patience.

9 *Tafsīr al-Saʿdī*, Surah *al-Baqarah*: verse 44.

HADITH 11
WE ARE ALL IN THE SAME SHIP

عن النعمان بن بشير رضي الله عنهما عن النبي ﷺ قال: 'مثل القائم على حدود الله والواقع فيها كمثل قوم استهموا على سفينة، فصار بعضهم أعلاها وبعضهم أسفلها، وكان الذين في أسفلها إذا استقوا من الماء مروا على من فوقهم فقالوا: لو أنا خرقنا في نصيبنا خرقًا ولم نؤذ من فوقنا ، فإن تركوهم وما أرادوا هلكوا وهلكوا جميعًا، وإن أخذوا على أيديهم نجوا ونجوا جميعا' (رواه البخاري).

The Prophet, may Allah bless him and give him peace, said: 'The likeness of the one who observes the limits prescribed by Allah and that who transgresses them is like the people who get on board a ship after casting lots. Some of them are in its lower deck and some of them in its upper deck. Those who are in its lower deck, when they require water, go to the occupants of the upper deck, and say to them: "If we make a hole in the bottom of the ship, we shall not harm you." If they (the occupants of the upper deck) leave them to carry out their design they will all be drowned. But if they do not let them go ahead with their plan, all of them will remain safe.'

COMMENTARY

This hadith builds on the previous one and uses a powerful analogy to show the impact of indifference among the righteous to the violations that transgress the boundaries of Allah. In the ship of society, those on the upper deck happen to have more knowledge, a broader perspective, and can see the big picture. Those on the bottom deck, even if they act with good intentions, want to take shortcuts and think outside the box. This is not surprising at all, once we realize how diverse people are in terms of their intellectual backgrounds and educational levels. Some may not have the same access to knowledge, and, even when they do, they tend to break the rules and challenge any type of authority thoughtlessly. So, the hadith is really posing the question to the believing men and women on the upper deck of that ship: are they going to abandon their responsibility, and leave it up to the whims and desires of the ignorant? Are they going to mind their own business? Or, are they going to consider it their business to save all the community members from such transgressions?

The following hadith and prophecy sheds some light on the consequences of some violations and sins, especially when they are normalized and publicized:

> *The Messenger of Allah, may Allah bless him and give him peace, came to us one day and said: O people of* Muhājirūn *[those who migrated from Makkah to Madinah], I warn you against five impending calamities and I ask Allah to protect you from even living long enough to witness them:*
>
> *When people openly and publicly commit the sins of adultery and fornication, then all kinds of plagues and diseases that were not known amongst people before will become widespread.*
>
> *And when merchants cheat in measures, weights, and scales in business, they will be afflicted with years of poverty, lack of basic needs, and extreme injustice from those in power.*

And when the rich deprive the poor of the charity that has to be taken from their wealth, then the same people will be deprived of rain coming from the skies. And were it not for the innocent animals and the cattle, these people would never witness any rain in their lives.

And as for those who break the oath that was given to Allah and His Messenger, Allah will cause an enemy to be sent upon them, and they will steal some of the resources to which they were entitled.

And when their leaders and governors do not rule by what Allah, glorified and exalted is He, has ordained, and start picking and choosing from the revelation that was sent down to them, Allah will cause conflicts and divisions to separate them. (Ibn Mājah)

It is important to emphasize that the hadith at hand does not negate the justice and mercy of Allah, for He does not burden a soul with the sin of another. However, the following hadith shows that such worldly punishment may befall on the whole community in the worldly life, while in the Hereafter the righteous will be saved by the mercy of Allah:

When evil appears in a land, Allah will send His destruction to its people. 'Ā'ishah, may Allah be pleased with her, asked, 'Even if they had among them worshippers?' And the Prophet, may Allah bless him and give him peace, answered, 'Yes, but then the righteous will be enveloped with the mercy of Allah.' (Aḥmad)

ACTION ITEMS AND FURTHER DISCUSSION

1. This hadith can inspire the artists in our community to unleash their creativity and communicate Islam's worldview on activism and *naṣīḥah*. Think about the details of the image of the ship of society, and the scene that the Prophet of Allah, may Allah bless him and give him peace, portrayed. What is the significance of using the analogy of the ship? What about the other elements of the scene that could be added to that analogy, such as the waves, wind, and ocean? How do people behave in a shared space whether they are feeling endangered or not? And what are the questions that could come to mind if one is a *ṣāliḥ* versus a *muṣliḥ*?

2. Reflect on the following verse which compliments and enforces the theme presented in this hadith:

   Beware of discord that harms not only the wrongdoers among you: know that God is severe in His punishment. (al-Anfāl 8: 25)

3. This hadith highlights a very important dimension of *naṣīḥah*. The two parties involved, the one giving and the other receiving the advice, are both in the same ship. Both experience the same temptations, social influences, and potential consequences, and both want the best for all passengers. By realizing that we are both in the same boat we avoid

common pitfalls, such as the one being advised, feeling defensive, or the preacher acting out of self-righteousness. Instead, by showing empathy and humility, the people of knowledge help both parties see the bigger picture and care for the whole ship, regardless of who is giving advice or receiving it. The advice given by Prophet Ibrāhīm to his father is key in this regard:

Father, knowledge that has not reached you has come to me, so follow me: I will guide you to an even path. (Maryam 19: 43)

4. Even if we fail to stop evil from happening, we at least have done our part, as portrayed in the story of the people of the Sabbath:

How, when some of them asked [their preachers], 'Why do you bother preaching to people God will destroy, or at least punish severely?' [The preachers] answered, 'In order to be free from your Lord's blame, and so that they may perhaps take heed.' (al-Aʿrāf 7: 164)

CHAPTER 3

THE WHAT [2]

THE POLITICAL RESPONSIBILITY OF MUSLIM ACTIVISTS

AS MUSLIMS, OUR faith invites us, in addition to serving our community and tending for its needs, to stand up against any form of oppression and injustice. Our ethical responsibility as caretakers of God's earth, as well as the last nation that was brought out to mankind, encourages us to consider the duties of civic engagement and political activism seriously.[10] This can be considered

10 Omar Suleiman, 'Faithful Activism: A Sunnah Framework', *Yaqeen Institute for Islamic Research*, Yaqeen Institute for Islamic Research, 9 March 2020, https://yaqeeninstitute.org/omar-suleiman/faithful-activism-a-sunnah-framework, (accessed December 2021).

as a complimentary requirement to the commandments of preaching Islam (*da'wah*), enjoining good, and forbidding evil (*al-amr bi'l-ma'rūf wa'l-nahy 'an al-munkar*):

> **You are the best nation produced [as an example] for mankind. You enjoin what is right and forbid what is wrong and believe in Allah.** (Āl 'Imrān 3: 110)

This *ayah* demonstrates that what makes our nation special is not some God-given privilege due to race, language, or culture. Instead, it is dependent on our fulfilment of the different aspects and dimensions of *da'wah* and activism (please refer to the Introduction of the above mentioned article for more insight on the definition of activism according to Islamic principles). A more specific instruction on the *ma'rūf* that Allah encourages us to enjoin and the *munkar* that Allah calls us to forbid is provided in Surah *al-Naḥl*: **God commands justice, doing good, and generosity towards relatives and He forbids what is shameful, blameworthy, and oppressive. He teaches you, so that you may take heed.** (al-Naḥl 16: 90)

According to Ibn 'Āshūr,[11] justice (*'adl*) is to give the bare minimum of rights when due, and it encompasses:

- Justice towards one's self, as when Allah says, **Do not contribute to your destruction with your own hands** (*al-Baqarah* 2: 159), by prohibiting intoxicants.
- Justice towards our Creator, by acknowledging His attributes and fulfilling our duties towards Him.

11 *Al-Taḥrir Wa'l-Tanwīr*, Ibn 'Āshūr Surah *al-Naḥl,* āyah 90.

- Justice towards the rest of creation, in our social and family circles, in both our speech and our actions Allah says: **And when you speak [i.e., testify], be just, even if [it concerns] a near relative,** (al-An'ām 6:152) and **when you judge between people to judge with justice.** (al-Nisā' 4:58) And if justice is the bare minimum that a Muslim should give when it's due, then excellence (*iḥsān*) is the maximum: it encompasses excellence in worshipping Allah as though one can see Him (as in the famous hadith of Jibrīl), as well as excellence in dealing with people, especially when no social norm or right invites us to do so. *Iḥsān* and justice are particularly important when it comes to our relatives, as the social justice framework in Islam starts with and focuses especially on our direct and extended families and relatives.

At the same time, Allah forbids three specific acts of injustice and sins that people may commit towards themselves, their families, or communities: Lewdness and indecency (*faḥshā'*), which refers to committing or spreading morally inappropriate actions and behaviour, such as adultery and fornication—clearly, such acts threaten the basic unit of society, the family, that Muslims are told by Allah to protect; recognized evil (*munkar*), which refers to the disagreeable and objectionable acts that human beings with sound minds and hearts reject and abhor (see hadith 12 for more insight);[12] rebellion and aggression (*baghy*) against Allah and

12 Abdur Rashid Siddiqui, *Qur'anic Keywords: A Reference Guide*, (Kube, 2015).

His commands, or against the innocent, the weak, and the oppressed segment of a community.

Another Qur'anic word that also goes in line with activism is reform (*iṣlāḥ*) which was used by Prophet Shuʿayb:

> **And I do not intend to differ from you in that which I have forbidden you. I only intend reform as much as I am able. And my success is not but through Allah. Upon him I have relied, and to Him I return.** (Hūd 11: 88)

His speech to his community is very relevant to Muslim activists. Prophet Shuʿayb, peace be upon him, announced that he would lead by example and practise what he preached. He also understands that his influence may be limited, but still strives to maximize his potential and initiate reform within his capacity. He also affirms his belief and trust in Allah that no change or success in his mission can be attained without Allah's approval and will.

In this chapter, we explore some of the hadith that can provide guidance towards establishing a framework for activism driven by Islamic principles. While the hadith in this chapter focus on the scope or approach—*the what*—those in Chapter 6 compliment this chapter with insight on the *fiqh* and the guidelines—*the how*.

HADITH 12
RESISTING CORRUPTION BY ALL MEANS POSSIBLE

عَنْ أَبِي سَعِيدٍ الْخُدْرِيِّ رَضِيَ اللهُ عَنْهُ قَالَ سَمِعْت رَسُولَ اللَّهِ صلى الله عليه و سلم يَقُولُ: 'مَنْ رَأَى مِنْكُمْ مُنْكَرًا فَلْيُغَيِّرْهُ بِيَدِهِ، فَإِنْ لَمْ يَسْتَطِعْ فَبِلِسَانِهِ، فَإِنْ لَمْ يَسْتَطِعْ فَبِقَلْبِهِ، وَذَلِكَ أَضْعَفُ الْإِيمَانِ' .

Abū Sa'īd al-Khudrī narrates that, 'I heard the Messenger of Allah, may Allah bless him and give him peace, say: "If one of you sees something wrong, let him change it with his hand; if he cannot, then with his tongue; if he cannot, then with his heart and this is the weakest level of faith."' (Muslim)

COMMENTARY

This hadith is a cornerstone of this whole collection of 40 hadith on community service and activism, as it sets the foundation upon which activism is viewed and taught in Islam. It teaches the essence of changing evil (*taghyīr al-munkar*) which can be paralleled to the verse *al 'Imran* 3: 110 cited earlier in this chapter.

Linguistically, *ma'rūf* is derived from the root *'arafa*, which is used in the context of recognizing and perceiving something. Hence, *ma'ruf* is that which is well-known, universally recognized, and generally accepted.[13] When used in the Qur'anic context, *ma'rūf* refers to good deeds that human beings recognize as wholesome and desirable. Examples include charitable acts, supporting the destitute, and establishing peace and harmony in a community.

Munkar is the opposite of *ma'ruf*, it shares the same root with other words that have meanings of denial, ignorance, and insignificance. In a sense, it refers to acts or behaviour that are disagreeable, objectionable, and detestable. Examples include abuse, pride, miserliness, infidelity, and oppression.

So, first of all, one has to identify a *munkar*, as defined and recognized by the laws of Allah, and as taught by scholars of the religion. Then comes the responsibility of protecting oneself and society from its impact, depending on each person's capacity and circle of influence. For a ruler or a decision-maker in a leadership position, this may be done by hand—by using one's official authority to rectify the situation. For most of the population, this may be achieved through one's tongue—by raising awareness, advocacy, and speaking out. In the absence of an environment of free speech, the weakest form of challenging evil is to reject it in one's heart. This entails that one should not be conditioned

---

13 Clearly, the notion of what's *ma'rūf* and what's *munkar* is not relative or subjective in Islam, but is defined by the Qur'an and the Sunnah. This may not be obvious in a world filled with post-modernist thought processes, and the reader is referred to the works of Sh. Suleiman Hani that address such misconception, such as this article: Suleiman Hani, 'Postmodernism and Truth', *The Message International*, ICNA Publication, 10 February 2021, https://messageinternational.org/community/postmodernism-and-truth/ (accessed 14 December 2021).

to accept it and normalize it, even if no outward or physical action can be done.

Some Muslims may take this hadith as an open invitation to enforce change in people's behaviour, which unfortunately has become a stereotype in the minds of some religious Muslims. However, the hadith clearly instructs us on what to do in cases where you *could not* change the wrongdoing. Therefore, it is of the essence to understand one's position in society and the likelihood of inducing real change in the lens of this hadith. Ibn al-Qayyim, may Allah have mercy on him, gave a profound breakdown of the situations associated with attempting to change evil, as well as the appropriate method in each case:[14]

Case 1: When you know that you can remove the evil completely and replace it with that which is good. For example, parents enforcing firm rules on their children in order to change a bad habit and replace it with a good one, or campaigning for a law that removes injustice from political prisoners.

Case 2: When you can reduce the harm of an act of wrongdoing, even if it was not eradicated. As an example, advising someone to avoid drinking alcohol in public, or partially lifting sanctions from a troubled Muslim region.

Case 3: When you know that attempting to correct a certain situation may result in a situation of equal harm. As an example, warning a parent about some wrong decisions

14 Ibn al-Qayyim, *Iʿlām al-Muwaqqiʿīn.*

taken in raising their children in a manner that may result in conflict with their spouse. An example from political activism might be to lobby for a policy or party that protects human rights in one country but compromises those same rights in another.

Case 4: When the act of trying to correct a wrongdoing results in greater harm. For example, when knowing in advance that advising someone to stop a sin may cause them to become rebellious and eventually spread it amongst others. Another example would be to boycott a politician or a party as a way of expressing discontentment with their policies that may result in turning them against the whole cause of supporting the Muslim community.

Ibn al-Qayyim suggested that enjoining good and forbidding evil is mandatory in the first two cases, requires careful assessment in the third one, and is completely *forbidden* in the fourth case. Wisdom, knowledge, and sound leadership are prerequisites to understand and apply this hadith , as we will see below in the remaining parts of this book.

SUGGESTED ACTION ITEMS

1. Reflect on the following three stories from Surah *al-Kahf* (surah 18), and the different methods of changing evil that can be considered as implementations of this hadith:
   a. The youth of the cave, and how they rejected the evil in their hearts and chose to escape any confrontation with their community.

b. The friend of the man with two gardens, who chose to give verbal advice to warn against the obsession with materialism that his friend had.
c. Dhū'l-Qarnayn, who was given immense political power and unmatched military resources, and how he used them to enforce real change in the lives of people.

2. This hadith is much needed for those sincere brothers and sisters who get overwhelmed by the amount of work needed to be done by Muslim activists, on multiple fronts, towards affecting even a small noticeable change. They may follow the news of killing and destruction in numerous countries around the Muslim world. They may experience a decline in the moral compass of a society affecting even the closest of their friends and family members. They may get discouraged from any involvement in the political process after they realize the limited impact of their engagement. All that may turn the sincerest members of the community to passive observers who just complain about the situation. Instead, Prophet Muhammad, may Allah bless him and give him peace, quickly shifts our attention to what we *can do* and *influence* with the few words 'if he cannot, then ...' More discussion on this specific point will be given in hadith 31.

3. This hadith is used as evidence by many scholars in the west to justify and even encourage participation

in democratic elections as a means of reducing or eliminating harm. Voting, in essence, is a form of changing evil through political power—by the hand—as well as through advocacy—by the tongue. Clearly, participation in a democratic election may feel uncomfortable for the God-conscious Muslim voter, for a number of reasons:

a. The feeling of being held responsible for the unfavourable positions that such candidates may hold. Voting may be seen as a form of endorsement for a candidate or a party's policies and even approval of the whole system.
b. The concern that such a candidate may deceive the Muslim community and end up causing more harm than good.
c. The assumption that it is safer, due to one's faith, to stay away from the whole process.

For these reasons, it is essential that Muslim activists and organizers base their decisions on rulings of credible scholarly bodies.[15] Such bodies have researched in full and contextualized well-known *fiqh* maxims, such as:

- *Ahwan al-ḍararayn*: Accepting the lesser evil to remove a greater one.
- *Lā Ḍarar Wa Lā Ḍirār*: Do not cause harm or return harm [Ibn Mājah]

15 Dr Muwaffaq Ghalayini, *Sharia Guidelines for Political engagement in America* (AMJA 2006).

- *Al-naẓar fi'l-ma'ālāt*: Taking into consideration the final consequences of one's actions.

According to scholarly bodies such as the Assembly of Muslim Jurists of America (AMJA), voting is not a complete endorsement of a candidate or a governing system, but a means to decrease harm in society and the world. Moreover, one is not held accountable if he or she votes for a candidate who does evil later on or changes their views.

4. The hadith at hand serves as evidence for using boycotting as a sign of disapproval, since participation may be a form of endorsement, which negates the essence of rejecting the *munkar* in one's heart. However, a counter argument may be given that participation and being at the table is an opportunity to speak out against other injustices. It may be very hard to draw a clear line between what is permissible and what is not in these cases, and thus arises the need for trusted scholars who understand both the religious rulings and the full political situation at hand. The Qur'an provides some clear examples of when to boycott certain discussions and gatherings that are situations of clear blasphemy against Allah and His revelation:

   If you hear people denying and ridiculing God's revelation, do not sit with them unless they start to talk of other things, or else you yourselves will become like them. (al-Nisā' 4: 140)

HADITH 13
THE HIGHEST LEVEL OF JIHAD

عَنْ أَبِي سَعِيدٍ الْخُدْرِيِّ، قَالَ قَالَ رَسُولُ اللَّهِ صلى الله عليه وسلم ' أَفْضَلُ الْجِهَادِ كَلِمَةُ عَدْلٍ عِنْدَ سُلْطَانٍ جَائِرٍ ' . أَوْ ' أَمِيرٍ جَائِرٍ ' (أبو داود)

Abū Sa'īd al-Khudrī narrated that the Messenger of Allah, may Allah bless him and give him peace, said: 'The best form of jihad (striving and struggling in the path of God) is to speak the word of truth in the face of an oppressor.' (Abū Dāwūd)

COMMENTARY

This famous hadith on speaking truth to power embodies multiple elements of activism principles in Islam: attempting to change evil with one's tongue (hadith 12), giving advice to the ruler (hadith 24), while fully trusting that the consequences are in the hands of Allah (hadith 5). It highlights the power of words as a means of change, even when someone does not have the political power to back it up. It brings to our attention the importance of taking a stand and adopting a courageous position in life, even if we do not believe it will reap immediate tangible benefits. At the end of the day, we are seeking Allah's pleasure by submitting to His commands, and we strongly believe that it is He who can bring real change to this earth filled with injustice. Allah may cause the oppressor to rethink his injustices or cast fear into his heart due to a few words that might otherwise be deemed ineffective. Allah may cause these words to influence those who succeed an oppressor, or encourage others to speak out who may be more successful. We can never know for sure where and how change will happen, and that is why we should rely on Allah Almighty, while we fulfil His commands to the best of our ability.[16]

From a linguistic perspective, the Arabic word *jihad* means to exert effort to resist harm and evil. This jihad could be against one's whims and ill-thoughts (*jihād al-nafs*; *al-Shuʿarā'* 26: 69), or war against oppression and persecution (*al-Tawbah* 9: 41). Jihad in the Qur'an is also mentioned in reference to debating false ideologies and belief systems through argument (*al-Furqān* 25: 52). After this quick overview of the different contexts and dimensions of jihad, one might ask: why is speaking truth to power considered a higher form of jihad?

Some scholars (like Imam al-Khaṭṭābī) mentioned that those in the battlefield experience contradicting emotions of fear of defeat and hope in victory. However, the one who speaks truth to a tyrant is mainly overwhelmed by fear, and thus his or her jihad represents a higher level of sacrifice. Imam al-Ṭaybī added that the oppression of a tyrant affects a larger number of people under him. Thus, resisting his oppression brings a great amount of benefit to the masses, when compared to fighting an enemy in a justified war.

Some scholars consider that this hadith connects all dimensions of jihad together, especially starting with *jihād al-nafs*.[17] When a believer challenges an oppressor, they are

16 Suleiman, O. *40 on Justice*, (Kube Publishing, 2020).
17 Suleiman, O. *40 on Justice*, (Kube Publishing, 2020).

striving against their own fears and weaknesses in addition to the struggle against the oppressor. This weakness, which is rooted in having poor faith in Allah and mistrust in His ability and His wisdom, is the first evil that should be removed from the hearts of believers.

Fighting in the battlefield, despite the risk of losing one's life, has its own worldly benefits, such as bragging and priding oneself for bravery, possession of spoils of war, among others. All of this disappears when one is challenging an oppressor with strong unsolicited advice. This is another reason that makes speaking truth to power a higher and more noble form of jihad. By the same token, Muslim activists should maintain their sincerity in civic engagement by ensuring that they do not seek any political gain or fame from speaking truth to power (as in hadith 1 and 2).

ACTION ITEMS BASED ON THE HADITH OF JIHAD

1. A Muslim community shall not surrender to their fears and stop fulfilling this important duty and responsibility of speaking truth to power, especially in any country where the right to freedom of expression is granted. The Prophet, may Allah bless him and give him peace, warns such people in this hadith:

'When people from my nation reach a point where they fear facing oppressors with their oppression, then there is no more hope left for them.' (al-Ḥākim)[18]

2. On the other hand, some leaders, intellectuals, or scholars may not fear for their lives but care for their popularity. They try to avoid displeasing those from above, such as their rulers or politicians, or those from below in the forms of their audience and common folk. Rulers do not wish their authority to be challenged, while the masses sometimes prefer reckless speech that only curses oppression and provides short-term outlets for their anger and frustration. A true scholar and activist should not be persuaded by either of these, and should try to fulfil this *ayah*: **Those who deliver God's messages and fear only Him and no other: God's reckoning is enough.** (al-Aḥzāb 33: 39)

3. This hadith should not be understood only in a political sense. Sometimes within our social circles we have oppressive leaders, systems and cultures that need to be challenged. Speaking out against a discriminating employer, an abusive family member, or inappropriate social norms are also avenues of jihad that a believer should strive to fulfil.

18 There is a little debate and disagreement between scholars on the authenticity of this report.

HADITH 14
CHOOSE YOUR BATTLES

عَنْ عَائِشَةَ، قَالَتْ قَالَ لِي رَسُولُ اللَّهِ صلى الله عليه وسلم ' لَوْلاَ حَدَاثَةُ عَهْدِ قَوْمِكِ بِالْكُفْرِ لَنَقَضْتُ الْكَعْبَةَ وَلَجَعَلْتُهَا عَلَى أَسَاسِ إِبْرَاهِيمَ فَإِنَّ قُرَيْشًا حِينَ بَنَتِ الْبَيْتَ اسْتَقْصَرَتْ وَلَجَعَلْتُ لَهَا خَلْفًا ' .(مسلم)

ʿĀʾishah narrated that the Messenger of Allah, may Allah bless him and give him peace, said to me: 'I would have demolished the Kaaba and rebuilt it on the foundations that were laid down by Ibrahim were it not due to the fact that your community have only recently left their disbelief. For when Quraysh built the Kaaba, they fell short in finalising its complete structure. Moreover, I would have built a door in it from the rear.' (Muslim)

COMMENTARY

By now, Muslim activists should realize their responsibility to speak truth to power, and to resist *munkar*, as appropriate to the situation at hand, either with their hand or tongue or at least in their hearts (see the commentary under hadith 12 above). However, one cannot resist all wrongdoing at once, and we need to examine (i) our potential and capacity and (ii) the order of priorities with the issues at hand. This starts with setting realistic expectations on the change that we want to see, focusing on high-impact areas, and deferring matters that are beyond our control.

The hadith at hand gives an example of the 'principled pragmatism' that the Messenger of Allah, may Allah bless him and give him peace, showed after the conquest of Makkah. The timing of this narration shows that his decision to keep the perceived wrong structure of the Kaaba did not coincide with a moment of political weakness and religious persecution. On the contrary, the Muslim community was at the pinnacle of its military ascendancy, and the Messenger of Allah held unquestionable political authority over all of Arabia. He could have easily ordered the rearrangement of the Kaaba's foundations, especially after having destroyed the 360 idols that surrounded it. Instead, and as guided by revelation, he set an example to all leaders on wisdom, strategic thinking, and prioritization.

It is also essential to note that Imam al-Bukhārī narrated this hadith under the heading, 'The Chapter on leaving some options unattended for the fear of misunderstanding from the masses, which may lead them to fall into a bigger mistake.' Ibn Ḥajar comments on this hadith in the following way:

> In this hadith there is guidance for the leader to accommodate the people as much as possible, and consider how they perceive certain issues and what may cause them to harm their own material or spiritual affairs.

ACTION ITEMS

1. Reflect on the following statement of Ibn Taymiyyah:

   The epitome of piety is when one can recognize the better out of two good choices, and the worst out of two bad choices. In addition, one should realize that the Shariah is based on attaining most or all of the benefits while minimizing or completely eliminating harm. Those who do not act based on balancing benefit and harm may fall short in completing their obligations or end up committing some violations.[19]

2. Many incidents in the *Sīrah* of Prophet Muhammad, may Allah bless him and give him peace, highlight this gradual approach that Islam followed in education (*tarbiyah*). An example is the gradual steps that Allah revealed in the prohibition of alcohol, teaching that alcohol's harms outweighed its benefits:

   They ask you [Prophet] about intoxicants and gambling, say: 'There is great sin in both, and some benefit for people: the sin is greater than the benefit. (al-Baqarah 2: 219)

   The Qur'an also forbade the Companions to pray while drunk:

19 Ibn Taymiyyah, *Majmū' al-Fatāwā*.

You who believe, do not come anywhere near the prayer if you are intoxicated, not until you know what you are saying. (al-Nisā' 4: 43)

Eventually, the Qur'an revealed an explicit command to completely avoid alcohol, with detailed listing of its harmful effects on the individual and society:

You who believe, intoxicants and gambling, idolatrous practices, and [divining with] arrows are repugnant acts—Satan's doing—shun them so that you may prosper. (al-Mā'idah 5: 90)

Activists and educators should ensure that their approach in reforming and educating a community starts with instilling faith, consciousness of Allah and accountability before Allah as a pre-requisite to teaching the commandments of Islam.

3. The following story from the life of Prophets Musa and Harun, may Allah bless them and give them peace, show us the different yet complimentary approaches that these two great messengers have and how they differed in addressing their community's issues. Musa came back after a long trip and saw his community worshipping the calf. He rebuked his brother Harun, assuming that he did not try to stop them from idolatry. The Qur'an narrates that discussion between the two great Prophets:

Musa said, 'When you realized they had gone astray, what prevented you, Harun, from coming after me? How could you disobey my orders?' [Harun] said, 'O son of my mother, do not seize [me] by my beard or by my head. Indeed, I feared that you would say, "You caused division among the Children of Israel, and you did not observe [or await] my word."' (Ṭa-Ha 20: 92-94)

It is instrumental to note here that Prophet Harun did not approve his community's worship of the calf, and it is wrong to assume that he preferred their unity over their *tawḥīd*. What really happened is that he issued a warning to them and tried to change the evil with his tongue, and they attempted to kill him for that. This caused him to switch his strategy and try to keep them together and not wander in the desert, until Mūsā came back and addressed the issue. That said, Muslims should not approve everything and anything under the banner of choosing our battles, and should ensure that our activism does not result in abandoning Allah's clear commands.

HADITH 15
POSITIVE INTERACTION WITH OTHER CULTURES

عَنِ ابْنِ عَبَّاسٍ رضى الله عنهما قَالَ لَمَّا قَدِمَ رَسُولُ اللَّهِ صلى الله عليه وسلم الْمَدِينَةَ، وَالْيَهُودُ تَصُومُ عَاشُورَاءَ، فَسَأَلَهُمْ، فَقَالُوا هَذَا الْيَوْمُ الَّذِي ظَهَرَ فِيهِ

مُوسَى عَلَى فِرْعَوْنَ، فَقَالَ النَّبِيُّ صلى الله عليه وسلم ' نَحْنُ أَوْلَى بِمُوسَى مِنْهُمْ فَصُومُوهُ '. (البخاري)

When Allah's Messenger, may Allah bless him and give him peace, arrived in Madinah, he found the Jews observing the fast on the day of 'Ashura (10th Muḥarram). The Prophet, may Allah bless him and give him peace, asked them about it and they replied, 'This is the day when Musa became victorious over Pharaoh.' The Prophet, may Allah bless him and give him peace, commented by saying, 'We are the true followers of Mūsā, more than them, so fast on this day.' (Bukhārī)

COMMENTARY

This hadith reflects the political reality of the Muslim community in Madinah, particularly with respect to relations with the Jewish community. Muslims shared many traits with the Jews, both being People of the Book, as opposed to the pagan Arabs who shared culture and language with the Muslims but differed in religion. However, this closeness in religion came with some clashes: the Jews expected the final messenger of God to be from their lineage, and did not appreciate the fact that Prophet Muhammad, may Allah bless him and give him peace, was Arab. This caused some rivalry and soft tension in Madinah, which was elevated into political turmoil and eventually to military conflict.

Despite the rivalry, the Messenger of Allah, may Allah bless him and give him peace, acknowledged the tradition of celebrating Mūsā's victory against the oppression of the Pharaoh. He did not let the political climate distract him from endorsing the legacy of Musa, and the fact that 'Muslims deserve to follow Musa more than them'!

This is a really important slogan for Muslims to adopt. When it comes to matters that are core to Islamic principles (such as social justice), a Muslim's political calling and agenda does not recognize political or racial boundaries. We simply align with the side of truth and justice, regardless of where that side is:

> **Believers! Stand firm for Allah and bear true testimony. Do not let the hatred of a people lead you to injustice. Be just! That is closer to righteousness.** (al-Mā'idah 5: 8)

Clearly, such hadith should not be understood as open permission to follow and adopt every value that other groups or faiths may teach or preach just because it is thought to be good. Such a misunderstanding, enabled by a defeatist mindset and a desire for assimilation at any cost, may open the door to compromising our Islamic values and identity. In fact, the Messenger of Allah, may Allah bless him and give him peace, later commanded the believers to fast one day before or after the Day of 'Āshūrā', for the sole purpose of keeping some distinction from the Jewish community (as the scholars interpreted). The message, rephrased, becomes that we ought to follow Mūsā more than the Jews, and we compete with them in good deeds by fasting an extra day.

ACTION ITEMS AND FURTHER DISCUSSIONS

1. Refer to trusted scholars when trying to examine the boundaries of interactions with other non-Muslim groups and organizations. In principle, Islam encourages collaboration on righteousness and piety and discourages cooperation on sin and transgression as in *al-Mā'idah* 5:2. We should seek true and genuine collaboration on areas that we agree on, such as family values, modesty, the legacy of the prophets that we believe in, and avoid a superficial display of interfaith unity. This should be done while recognizing our differences and without shying away from discussing them. Such collaboration does not necessarily result in endorsement or acceptance of other groups' ideologies or beliefs, particularly if the terms and conditions are clearly defined. In the midst of political organizing and community service projects, we should not lose sight of our calling as Muslims to invite others to the religion of Allah and the values that Islam brings to the table.

2. Reflect on the following hadith and statement from ʿAmr ibn al-ʿĀṣ (RA), which shows (i) the awareness and (ii) the recognition that the messenger of Allah, may Allah bless him and give him peace, and the Companions had for the cultural experiences of the Byzantine empire:

'Amr ibn al-'Āṣ (RA) narrates that he heard al-Mustawrid al-Qurashī (RA) saying:

I heard Allah's Messenger, may Allah bless him and give him peace, say, 'When the Day of Judgement comes, the Romans will form the majority of the world's population.' Amr responded by asking, 'Are you sure of your statement?' He said, 'I only say what I heard from Allah's Messenger himself, may Allah bless him and give him peace.' Thereupon 'Amr said, 'If your statement is accurate, then I know for a fact that they have four good qualities: They are the most patient of people during trials and tribulations, they immediately restore order after a calamity, they regroup themselves quickly to retaliate after being attacked, and they show immense goodness to the destitute, the orphaned and the weak.' Then 'Amr added, 'And they have a fifth good and beautiful quality: that they are the most likely of people to resist and stop kings from oppression.' (Muslim)

3. The discussion on exploring words of wisdom from other traditions and sources should not result in an open-ended invitation to adopt any foreign idea or concept, just because it may sound appealing or nice. Some Muslims with good intentions quote the following weak hadith and extrapolate a lot of meanings from it, 'Wisdom is the lost property of the believer: wherever he finds it, he is most deserving of it.' (Narrated by Tirmidhī, rated as very weak by al-Albānī)

Such a mindset may have detrimental long-term effects to the intellectual integrity of our Islamic teachings. After all, who defines what is wise and what is not, and by what measure should Muslims define their standards of morality and righteousness? In this day and age, Muslim activists are bombarded with a lot of appealing ideas, whether they are mentioned in a business text book, the biography of a successful leader, or a viral marketing campaign. Clearly, it will be inauthentic and even dangerous to incorporate whatever deep-sounding quote that we encounter as wisdom, and then use such weak narrations to justify such behaviour.

HADITH 16
MEDIA AND THE MUSLIM PUBLIC IMAGE

قَالَتْ عَائِشَةُ : فَسَمِعْتُ رَسُولَ اللَّهِ صَلَّى اللَّهُ عَلَيْهِ وَسَلَّمَ يَقُولُ لِحَسَّانَ : ' إِنَّ رُوحَ الْقُدُسِ لَا يَزَالُ يُؤَيِّدُكَ، مَا نَافَحْتَ عَنِ اللَّهِ وَرَسُولِهِ '. وَقَالَتْ : سَمِعْتُ رَسُولَ اللَّهِ صَلَّى اللَّهُ عَلَيْهِ وَسَلَّمَ يَقُولُ : ' هَجَاهُمْ حَسَّانُ، فَشَفَى وَاشْتَفَى '. (مسلم)

'Ā'ishah reported that the Messenger of Allah said to Ḥassān: 'Indeed the Holy Spirit (Angel Jibrīl) will send his support to you, so long as you keep on doing your work of fighting this battle of poetry on behalf of Allah and His Messenger.'
'Ā'ishah comments that she heard the Messenger of Allah saying later: 'Ḥassān used his satire against the disbelievers,

and satisfied and healed the feelings of the believers.' (Muslim)[20]

COMMENTARY

Historically, poetry was known to be the most powerful medium for the Arabs. The poems that went viral during the *Jāhiliyyah*, the pre-Islamic period of Ignorance, were known as the suspended odes (*al-mua'llaqāt*) because they were posted on the walls of the Kaaba. Eloquent speech always used its charm in moving the masses, rallying people, and even building convictions beyond logical explanations and arguments. As narrated in another hadith: '*Some eloquent speech has a strong effect like magic on people.*' (Bukhārī)

The Quraysh used poetry on many occasions to defame the Messenger of Allah, may Allah bless him and give him peace, and attack his message. In a longer narration of the same hadith , he encouraged the Companions to use their talent and represent Islam in this war of words. The talent search led to Ḥassān ibn Thābit (RA), who got the lion's share of the prophetic prayers. Scholars build on this same narration to argue that any media work that defends the Prophet, may Allah bless him and give him peace, and introduces his message to the world can hope for a similar reward and blessing that Ḥassān ibn Thābit received.

There is another narration that provides, at length, the whereabouts of the creation of the poem that Hassan used to

20 Original hadith narration rephrased and reworded for brevity and context.

attack the Quraysh, it shows how Abū Bakr al-Ṣiddīq, may Allah be pleased with him, an expert in the lineages of the Quraysh tribes, teamed up with Ḥasan, the acclaimed poet, to provide a fascinating media production project. The satire of Ḥassān was supposed to target the families of the arrogant leaders of the Quraysh and defame them, but without insulting the forefathers of the Prophet Muhammad himself. This required close attention to details from both creators, Ḥassān and Abū Bakr. Clearly, Ḥassān's poetry went viral, raised the spirits of the Muslim community, and caused the Quraysh leadership to rethink many times whether they would use propagandistic poetry again the Muslims again. It proved to be a powerful tool that—when used properly and in a measured way— served the Muslim cause and boosted Islam's presence in intellectual and cultural circles within Arabia.

Of course, the power of words and the influence of the media are tools that can be used in multiple ways, and that are unfortunately used by many to promote evil and mischief. The Qur'an tells us how many poets choose to corrupt and misguide the masses, but in the same passage affirms that there will always be righteous ones who will stand up for truth with their words:

> **And the poets—only the deviators follow them; Do you not see that in every valley they roam; And that they say what they do not do? Except those poets who believe and do righteous deeds and remember Allah often and defend the Muslims after they were wronged. And those who have wronged are going to know to what kind of return they will be returned.** (al-Shuʿarāʾ 26: 224-227)

FURTHER DISCUSSIONS

1. Muslim activists should be wary of the deceitful nature of the media and the public relations industry, ensuring to use them as a means and not as an end. Generally speaking, people in such domains favour political correctness, a glossy public image, and superficial style over substance, truthfulness, and righteousness. To the contrary, a Muslim's involvement in public affairs should be sincerely about guiding people to the truth and supporting the oppressed and the weak. The previously mentioned *āyah* (*al-Shuʿarāʾ* 26: 224-227) should serve as a reminder that most people may use such tools for promoting lies and injustice.

2. The hadith at hand highlights an interesting tactic that the Messenger of Allah, may Allah bless him and give him peace, used against those who defamed him. In general, the Muslims are instructed to respond to insults with wisdom and to repel evil with good as in *Fuṣṣilat* 41: 34, and avoid insulting the beliefs of others:

   Believers, do not revile those they call on beside God in case they, in their hostility and ignorance, revile God. (al-Anʿām 6: 108)

   However, we see how Ḥassān was praised for using his strong and offensive satire against the Quraysh and their lineage. It is important to learn from the prophetic wisdom how to use the right approach at the right time. In Ḥassān's case, his poetry resulted in forcing the Quraysh to stop the back-and-forth poetry campaign, which is exactly what the Muslims wanted. Islam thrives better when enough time is given for the right ideas to be presented, and the poetry of Quraysh was not allowing that to happen. This is why the Qur'an gave permission, in some cases, for the Muslims to respond in a similar way to the offense that was initiated:

If you, believers, have to respond to an attack, make your response proportionate, but it is best to stand fast. (al-Naḥl 16: 126)

3. On multiple occasions, we see that Prophet Muhammad, may Allah bless him and give him peace, dealt with the public image of the Muslim community in a very delicate manner. Aside from basic tenants of the faith that one should not compromise, he cared for the way Islam was being viewed in public and how other people would interpret his actions. One example was the defamation from 'Abdullāh ibn Ubayy ibn Salūl, the leader of the hypocrites in Madinah, who once announced in public:

'By Allah, if we return to Madinah, the more honourable leader in it will expel the disgraceful one.' 'Umar ibn al-Khaṭṭāb, may Allah be pleased

with him, heard his statement and asked for permission from the Messenger of Allah, may Allah bless him and give him peace, to kill 'Abdullāh ibn Ubayy, 'O Allah's Messenger! Please let me chop off the head of this hypocrite!' But the Prophet Muhammad, may Allah bless him and give him peace, said, 'Leave him, lest the people say that Muhammad kills his Companions.' (Bukhārī and Muslim)

Ibn 'Āshūr (RA) commented on this incident: The Prophet, may Allah bless him and give him peace, chose not to kill the hypocrites in order to avoid a situation where newcomers to the faith start doubting their own safety. In general, the masses and especially those living outside Madinah did not get the full picture of what was happening inside it. This gave the voices of tribulations and confusion an easy opportunity to start another misinformation campaign against Islam.[21]

HADITH 17
CHALLENGE TRIBAL AND POLITICAL BOUNDARY LINES

عن أنس أنه قال: قال رسول الله صلى الله عليه وسلم: 'انصر أخاك ظالمًا أو مظلومًا' فقال رجل: يا رسول الله أنصره إذا كان مظلومًا أرأيت إن كان ظالمًا كيف أنصره؟ قال: 'تحجزه -أو تمنعه- من الظلم فإن ذلك نصره' (رواه البخاري).

21 *Tafsir al-Tahrir wa-al-tanwir*, Vol 10, Muhammad al-Tahir Ibn Ashur, (Dar al-Tunisiyah lil-Nashr, 1969)

> *Anas, may Allah be pleased with him, reported that the Messenger of Allah, may Allah bless him and give him peace, said: 'Support your brother whether he is an oppressor or is oppressed.' A man enquired, 'O Messenger of Allah! I can help him when he is oppressed, but how can I help him when he is an oppressor?' He, may Allah bless him and give him peace, said, 'You can keep him from committing oppression. That will be your helping him.'* (Bukhārī and Muslim)

COMMENTARY

Islam came to put an end to tribalism and blind following of a race, ethnicity, or political ideology. It defined a new relation between believers that was based on faith and submission to Allah without any other bias. The Prophet, may Allah bless him and give him peace, warned the believers against this:

> *Jundab ibn 'Abdullāh (RA) reported that the Messenger of Allah, may Allah bless him and give him peace, said, 'Whoever is killed under the banner of tribal solidarity* (aṣabiyyah), *who calls to tribalism or supports tribalism, then he has died upon ignorance.'* (Muslim)

This culture cannot be easily erased from any society or any community, and even when it came to the Companions, the Messenger, may Allah bless him and give him peace, had to deal with that legacy of the Age of Ignorance (*Jāhiliyyah*). In the *Sīrah*, we read of some incidents where the Companions were on the cusp of slipping back into internal conflict that would have reignited the civil war between the Aws and the Khazraj. This caused the Messenger of Allah, may Allah bless him and give him peace, to rebuke them staunchly, 'How can you resurrect the call of *Jāhiliyyah* even when I am still with you?'

Therefore, the Prophet, may Allah bless him and give him peace, used multiple methods to remove the deeply ingrained values of *Jāhiliyyah*. In the hadith at hand, the Messenger of Allah, may Allah bless him and give him peace, referenced a saying famed among the Arabs, but he reframed its meaning to convey the right Islamic understanding of brotherhood, truth and mutual support. Namely, support for your oppressing Muslim brother or sister can only happen if you advise them and stop their oppression. Support, victory, and brotherhood was lifted to a spiritual level beyond worldly measures. The Prophet, may Allah bless him and give him peace, did not try to change Islamic concepts and values to fit into the existing culture, but rather reframed those tribal dimensions of brotherhood and support in an Islamically acceptable manner.

This discussion is very relevant to Muslims trying to get involved in politics. In our attempts to bring our values of enjoining good and forbidding evil, and supporting the weak and the needy, we shall not change our language and values to conform with political party lines. In other words, we should do our best to 'Islamize' our political involvement and endeavours, and avoid, by all means, politicizing Islam to fit into a party's agenda.

How can we ensure that we are protected from changing our *din*? We should be reminded that politics is a means to an end. It is a tool to change the *munkar* and wrongdoing that a community's present situation manifests. Politics is imperfect like any other manmade system or tool, and has to be always used with discretion and care. We should resist the tendency to label our community or associate our values with any of the 'isms'.[22]

FURTHER DISCUSSION

1. Examine with an objective lens the political and social trends that take place in your community and in the world at large. Examine their assumptions and challenge the values that such movements adopt. In general, many causes that get popular, such as patriotism and feminism, may have an element of agreement with Islamic principles, such as loving one's country or protecting women from domestic abuse.[23] However, Muslim activists should not immediately buy into the superficial slogans

22 Suleiman, O, '*Faithful Activism: A Sunnah Framework*', a Publication by Yaqeen Institute, March 9th, 2020, https://yaqeeninstitute.org/omar-suleiman/faithful-activism-a-sunnah-framework, last accessed December 2021

23 Alkiek, T., Mogahed, D., Suleiman, O., and Brown, J. May 22, 2017, "Islam and Violence Against Women: A Critical Look at Domestic Violence and Honor Killings in the Muslim Community" https://yaqeeninstitute.org/tesneem-alkiek/islam-and-violence-against-women-a-critical-look-at-domestic-violence-and-honor-killings-in-the-muslim-community.

of any movement without looking carefully at its intellectual foundations. Refer to the expertise of scholars when determining whether aspects of these 'isms' align with Islamic values, and reflect on how you can use this hadith as an inspiration to articulate Islam's position on it.

2. Study the history and evolution of public taste and inclination towards certain trends: how the boundaries of modesty and chastity changed in the past, or how the public perception of certain forms of relationship such as homosexuality or paedophilia have changed, for example.

3. We see in the life and legacy of Muhammad Ali, may Allah have mercy on him, a true manifestation of this hadith. His true understanding of patriotism and supporting one's country did not include getting involved in an unjust war. Muhammad Ali stuck to the unpopular opinion of refusing to go to Vietnam, and by sticking to his principles, became an example of an athlete, a Muslim American, and a true patriot beyond the labels that the media of the time were using to define him and others.

CHAPTER 4

THE WHO

INSIDE YOUR TEAM: PROPHETIC WISDOM ON EMPOWERING AND LEADING A SUCCESSFUL TEAM

ONCE A GROUP is formed by either experienced veterans in the field or by passionate newcomers, it is very likely that its members will face the same universal challenges of teamwork: how to build a sustainable team, recruit the right person for the right task, establish synergy between members, and navigate differences in personality. Such issues—often referred to as people issues or internal politics—may threaten the fabric of the group, and result in a huge drain of time and resources, while removing the *barakah* and spiritual effectiveness of the group.

> **And obey Allah and His Messenger, and do not dispute and [thus] lose courage and [then] your strength would depart; and be patient. Indeed, Allah is with the patient.** (al-Anfāl 8: 46)

The maxim of joining forces and collaboration on all righteous causes is well established in the Qur'an:

> **And cooperate in righteousness and piety, but do not cooperate in sin and aggression. And fear Allah; indeed, Allah is severe in penalty.** (al-Mā'idah 5: 2)

The hadith in Chapter 4 are meant to equip activists and community workers with prophetic inspiration on the best practices to build and sustain teams. Please read with an intention to tap into the spiritual blessing (*barakah*) of being part of a congregation, follow the prophetic advice, and maximize the impact of your service to 27 times—the reward of praying in congregation—and even more!

HADITH 18
THE SCARCITY OF LEADERS

عَنْ عَبْدَ اللَّهِ بْنَ عُمَرَ رَضِيَ اللَّهُ عَنْهُمَا قَالَ : سَمِعْتُ رَسُولَ اللَّهِ صَلَّى اللَّهُ عَلَيْهِ وَسَلَّمَ يَقُولُ: ' إِنَّمَا النَّاسُ كَالْإِبِلِ الْمِائَةِ لَا تَكَادُ تَجِدُ فِيهَا رَاحِلَةً '
(البخاري و مسلم)

It was narrated from 'Abdullāh ibn 'Umar that the Messenger of Allah (may Allah bless him and give him peace) said: 'Finding truly authentic people is as rare as finding dependable camels:

out of a hundred, you may rarely find one that is worth taking on a long journey.' (Bukhārī and Muslim)

COMMENTARY

This hadith draws from the culture of the Arabian desert that the Messenger of Allah, may Allah bless him and give him peace, lived in. Before a traveller embarked on a long journey, it was essential to pick the right camel that could be entrusted in such a life-and-death situation. One may have to find that one rare camel out of a hundred that is smart, quick and easily managed. The scholars commented that this hadith applies to many areas in life (as in the case of choosing good friends). In the realm of community service and activism, this hadith invites the leadership in every organization to strive to recruit, train and retrain the right volunteers and invest in them. This is particularly important once we compare the amount of effort and planning that some institutes spend on raising funds compared with giving attention to raising *human capital.* Clearly, it is understandable that monetary funds are needed to sustain and expand the activities and services of a group. However, we should shift our mindset to appreciating the value of human resources: those who believe deeply in the cause of the group, are passionate about their work, and are willing to pour themselves into the work and put countless hours into it. This mindset was clear in the leadership of ʿUmar ibn al-Khaṭṭāb (RA), as is shown by the following story that was narrated by Zayd ibn Aslam on behalf of his father.

'Umar ibn al-Khaṭṭāb once asked those around him, 'If you were to make a wish, what would it be?' Some started saying, 'I wish that I had a house full of gold, so I could donate it in the path of Allah.' Another man said, 'I wish it was full of pearls and precious gems, so I could spend all of them in the path of Allah.'

Clearly, 'Umar was unimpressed by their answers, and kept asking them, keep imagining, keep thinking, until they said, 'O leader of the believers, we don't really know what to wish for!'

At which point he said: 'If it was for me, I wish that this room was full of real men like Abū 'Ubaydah ibn al-Jarrāḥ (RA), Mu'ādh ibn Jabal (RA), Sālim (RA) the servant of Abū Ḥudhayfah, and Ḥudhayfah ibn al-Yamān! (RA)'[24]

'Umar, may Allah be pleased with him, understood the value of these individuals who carried the torch of Islam to the major cities and countries of the world. Some were deep scholars who taught the masses the Qur'an and the hadith. Others were army commanders who were not seduced by worldly or political gains. If we are serious in following the footsteps of 'Umar ibn al-Khaṭṭāb, we shall have to go the extra mile to appreciate every single volunteer for what he or she does for our community.

24 *Siyar A'lām Al-Nubalā'*.

ACTION ITEMS

1. Focus on attracting and developing leaders with strong personalities, while empowering others to be excellent and proactive team players. Empower your volunteers and create the right culture to help them develop their skills. You can do that by shifting your definition of success from capitalist metrics, such as donations raised, or number of attendees in an event, to people-centred ones, such as the quality of the people who consider your organization as their second home.

2. The Arabs have a beautiful proverb on the importance on delegating tasks to the wise, 'Send a wise person on a mission and you will have less need to give instructions.' Clearly, such leaders do not need to be micromanaged, because they have both the passion and the know-how to complete their tasks.

3. Read Surah *al-Naml* with your team (Surah 27), and encourage them to reflect on the leadership qualities of Prophet Sulaymān, may Allah send him peace, and how he inspired others like the ant (27: 18) and the hoopoe (27: 20-24). This story serves as a monumental example of a motivated and organized community, from its tiniest and weakest members to its most influential ones.

4. While the hadith at hand confirms that leaders are a scarce and rare commodity, we should realize that they are always there. This is particularly true once we expand our search to include people outside the immediate circle of volunteers that we interact with. Many members in our community are gems that need to be discovered and empowered. Even when it comes to non-Muslims, the Prophet, may Allah bless him and give him peace, indicated how Islam brings the best out of their previously acquired character once they are guided to it. Abū Hurayrah (RA) reported:

   I heard the Messenger of Allah, may Allah bless him and give him peace, saying, 'People are like mines of gold and silver: the best of them in the Age of Ignorance are the best of them in Islam, so long as they have the proper religious understanding. And the souls are drafted soldiers: they come together upon what they recognize, and they differ upon what they reject.' (Muslim)

HADITH 19
AVOID MATERIALISTIC STANDARDS

عَنْ سَهْلٍ، قَالَ مَرَّ رَجُلٌ عَلَى رَسُولِ اللَّهِ صلى الله عليه وسلم فَقَالَ ‘ مَا تَقُولُونَ فِي هَذَا ’. قَالُوا حَرِيٌّ إِنْ خَطَبَ أَنْ يُنْكَحَ، وَإِنْ شَفَعَ أَنْ يُشَفَّعَ، وَإِنْ قَالَ أَنْ يُسْتَمَعَ. قَالَ ثُمَّ سَكَتَ فَمَرَّ رَجُلٌ مِنَ فُقَرَاءِ الْمُسْلِمِينَ فَقَالَ ‘ مَا تَقُولُونَ فِي هَذَا ’. قَالُوا حَرِيٌّ إِنْ خَطَبَ أَنْ لاَ يُنْكَحَ وَإِنْ شَفَعَ أَنْ لاَ يُشَفَّعَ،

وَإِنْ قَالَ أَنْ لاَ يُسْتَمَعَ. فَقَالَ رَسُولُ اللَّهِ صلى الله عليه وسلم ' هَذَا خَيْرٌ مِنْ مِلْءِ الأَرْضِ مِثْلَ هَذَا '.

Sahl narrates that a man passed by the Messenger of Allah, may Allah bless him and give him peace, while he was surrounded by his Companions. He asked them, 'What is your opinion about this man?' They replied, 'This person is from the elite and the noblest of people. If he ever proposes to a woman, the family will accept him right away, and if he were to intercede for someone, his intercession would definitely be granted, and if he were to give a speech, then everybody would listen and pay attention.' The Messenger of Allah (may Allah bless him and give him peace) remained silent, until another poor man passed by. He asked again, 'What is your opinion about this man?' So they replied, 'If this man proposed to a woman, the family would definitely reject him, and if he were to intercede for someone, his intercession would not be granted, and if he were to give a speech, no one would take him seriously or listen to him.' Afterwards, the Messenger of Allah, may Allah bless him and give him peace, said, 'This one is better in the sight of Allah than a whole world's worth like the first one.' (Bukhārī)

COMMENTARY

This hadith highlights yet another challenge in finding and recruiting the already scarce human resources for community service: the improper selection of leadership, and the materialistic standards that interfere with people's perception of talent and competence. Such misunderstanding may find its way to our community forums and organizations in different ways. In some cases, it could be blunt tribalism and nationalism that defines who is in and who is out. At other times, it may be the emphasis on academic credentials, advanced college degrees, or business success. Clearly, a leader in the Muslim community is expected to demonstrate some level of success in other areas of life. However, we should be careful about the criteria that go into defining success. For example, do we include one's relationship with his or her family as part of this criteria? What about being a role model in practising and preaching Islam? Or having a good balance between being firm and determined, while accommodating opposing viewpoints and uniting people?

In Surah *al-Baqarah* (Surah 2), Allah narrates a story from an earlier generation of the Israelites, and how they prepared themselves to go to battle. The story highlights a discussion that took place between the elite of that community and their prophet:

> **Their prophet said to them, 'God has now appointed Ṭālūt to be your king,' but they said, 'How can he be king over us when we have a greater right to rule than he? He does not even have great wealth.' He said, 'God has chosen him over you, and has given him great knowledge and stature. God grants His authority to whoever He pleases: God is magnanimous, all knowing.'** (al-Baqarah 2: 247)

The elite were so materialistic in their criteria that they only focused on wealth and, implicitly, social status as requirements for leadership. Instead, their prophet focused their attention on two qualities: knowledge and physical strength. It is interesting that the verse recognizes the physical strength of Ṭālūt as a valid qualification; it was not dismissed for being a materialist standard, especially in the context of a battlefield, and when exercised through knowledge and faith (as in hadith 34). By the same token, Prophet Mūsā, may Allah send him peace, was praised for having two noble qualities:

> **One of the women said, 'O my father, hire him. Indeed, the best one you can hire is the strong and the trustworthy.'** (al-Qaṣaṣ 28: 26)

This was mentioned after Mūsā helped the two women in Madyan and provided water for their sheep. This historic comment about Musa became the golden standard for hiring and recruiting people in Islam: strength and trustworthiness!

ACTION ITEMS

1. Inform your team and your community of the two hadith in Bukhari that attribute having a leadership crisis in the world, and in the Muslim community, to the imminence of the Day of Judgement:

   'When the affairs of the community are not handed to the right person, then you can anticipate that the Day of Judgement is very close.' (Bukhārī)

'I fear six things for you: the leadership of the foolish ones, and the spread of bloodshed, and the selling of kingship, and the cutting of the ties of kinship, and having people who take the Qur'an as a means of entertainment and melodies, and the abundance of corrupt police and informants.' (Bukhārī)

2. The discussion on righteousness as a quality for leadership should not be made as an excuse for mediocracy and incompetence. We shall not end up in the position, as a community, to choose spirituality over competence, for we should strive for both in our leaders. In fact, this dilemma is exactly the one that 'Umar ibn al-Khaṭṭāb, may Allah be pleased with him, made a profound supplication against: 'Oh Allah, I seek refuge in you from witnessing the perseverance of the sinner, and the powerlessness of the trustworthy.'

3. Create opportunities for the wealthy members of the community to be recognized and acknowledged for their contributions without the need for them to be placed in leadership positions unless worthy of them.

HADITH 20
CAN I ASK FOR LEADERSHIP?

عن أبي موسى الأشعري رضي الله عنه قال: دخلت على النبى صلى الله عليه وسلم أنا ورجلان من بني عمي، فقال أحدهما: يا رسول الله أمرنا على بعض ما ولاك الله، عز وجل، وقال الآخر مثل ذلك، فقال: 'إنا والله لا نولى هذا العمل أحدا سأله، أو أحدا حرص عليه' ((متفق عليه)) .

Abū Mūsā al-Ash'arī, may Allah be pleased with him, narrates that 'I met the Prophet, may Allah bless him and give him peace, along with two of my cousins. They said to him, "O Messenger of Allah, can you appoint us to lead some of the new lands which Allah Almighty has given you authority over?" The Messenger (may Allah bless him and give him peace) said, "By Allah, we do not give leadership to anyone who seeks it or contends for it."' (Bukhārī and Muslim)

COMMENTARY

As a general rule, a believer who aims to meet Allah in the Afterlife with a sound heart is encouraged to refrain from seeking positions of influence and fame. Islam encourages us to stay humble and keep our hearts in check to ensure a safer trip to the Hereafter:

> **We grant the Home in the Hereafter to those who do not seek superiority on earth or spread corruption: the happy ending is awarded to those who are mindful of God.** (al-Qaṣaṣ 28: 83)

Many scholars have interpreted the forementioned verse and hadith to conclude that it is disliked and even forbidden to actively seek a position of leadership and authority. Other narrations support this conclusion, such as the following hadith: *'O Abū Dharr! You know that you have a weak personality, and that leadership is a heavy responsibility, and it will only bring you disgrace and regret on the Day of Judgement, except for those who fulfil its rights and completely devote themselves to it.'* (Muslim)

On the other hand, a counterargument exists in Islam that encourages those amongst the believers who are trustworthy, both in spirituality and skills, to step up for leadership. This is particularly true in the presence of incompetent leaders who disregard the forementioned prophetic wisdom, and hence will be undeterred from filling critical positions in an organization. As an example, Prophet Yūsuf, may Allah bless him and give him peace, nominated himself to a governmental position in Egypt when he believed in his ability and qualifications:

> **Yusuf said, 'Appoint me over the storehouses of the land. Indeed, I will be a knowing guardian.'** (Yūsuf 12: 55)

Of course, this argument opens up another set of questions: who amongst the Muslim community is comparable to Yūsuf? And was this ruling of permissibility exclusive to a prophet who found himself in a corrupt nation?

Imam Nawawī, in his commentary on *Ṣaḥīḥ Muslim*, reconciled the two opinions by selecting an interpretive title for the chapter that narrates the aforementioned hadith of Abū Dharr: 'The chapter on the ruling of seeking a position of governance, and how it is disliked unless there is a necessity.' By doing so, he did not generalize the ruling of impermissibility in asking for a governance position, especially in cases of perceived necessity.

An interesting incident that supports this position is the story of Ziyād ibn al-Ḥārith al-Suda'ī, who invited his whole tribe to Islam and brought them to the Messenger of Allah, may Allah bless him and give him peace. After successfully completing his mission, he narrated, 'I asked him to appoint me as a leader of my people, and to confirm my appointment in an official letter, and the Messenger, may Allah bless him and give him peace, did so.'

Ibn al-Qayyim comments on this narration:

> This narration shows the permissibility of appointing a leader who asks for a position if he can prove his skills. Hence, the mere fact of seeking governance does not discredit the right person. And this does not contradict the other hadith 'We don't appoint over our affairs those who want it and strive for it', because the man from Suda'ī, Ziyād ibn al-Ḥārith, specifically asked to lead his people. He knew he was beloved to them, and they would obey him and follow his command. He also wanted their best interests by inviting them to accept Islam. On the other hand, those who asked for leadership in the first narration were only concerned with their personal benefit and interests, so the Prophet

> (may Allah bless him and give him peace) forbade them from it. So the Messenger of Allah appointed a leader for the greater good, and forbade another person from it also for the greater good.[25]

Al-Ghazālī gives a beautiful commentary on this:

> Those with limited understanding may assume that the different hadith on seeking leadership positions contradict one another, but this is not true at all: for the few individuals who are strong in their faith, they should not shy away from leadership; and for those who are weak, they should keep a distance from it, or otherwise their faith will be ruined. The strength mentioned here is defined by not being deluded by the materialistic life, or being driven by greed, or fearing anyone besides Allah. Those are the ones who made worldly life and other creations insignificant in their eyes. Those are the ones who conquered their lower-selves (*nafs*) and took control over their desires, and caused the Devil to give up on trying to seduce them. Those are the ones who are only moved by the truth, and only stopped from doing something because of the truth, even if they put their lives on the line. Those are the ones who ought to take leadership and governance positions in every time and place.[26]

---

25 Ibn Qayyim Al-Jawziyyah, *Zad al-maad*.
26 Al-Bukhari, *Iḥyā' 'Ulūm al-Dīn*.

ACTION ITEMS

1. Be proactive in addressing disputes over leadership positions. Invest in building the skills and the competency of your community, in addition to their spirituality, knowledge, and connection to Allah. Revive the values of responsibility, self-awareness, and servant-based leadership in your community. This can be done by sharing powerful stories from our rich Islamic history, such as this famous one about 'Umar ibn al-Khaṭṭāb during his last moments before he died: A suggestion was made to nominate 'Umar's son, 'Abdullāh, as the succeeding caliph for the Muslim *ummah*. Although 'Abdullāh's credibility was not in question, 'Umar famously retorted that: 'Is it not enough for one person from the family of al-Khaṭṭāb to carry this burden and be held responsible by His Lord?'

2. The right leadership should let every team member feel empowered and have a real sense of authority in his or her domain of excellence. This should empower activists to feel a sense of ownership and hopefully stop them from developing ambitions to become *the* leader, as they have the chance to maximize their potential within each role (refer to hadith 9).

3. Reflect on the following statement for Sufyān ibn 'Abbād, 'Those who seek a position of leadership before its time will cause it to flee from them.'

The implication here is that those who are sincere and competent in their work will be able to prove themselves. They should trust that Allah will facilitate the right environment and conditions for that to happen. On the other hand, if they crave power and work desperately to gain authority, this may remove all the Divine help and *barakah*, and cause tension and hatred in everyone's hearts.

HADITH 21
BE PATIENT WITH PEOPLE'S DRAMA

حَدَّثَنَا آدَمُ، قَالَ: حَدَّثَنَا شُعْبَةُ، عَنِ الأَعْمَشِ، عَنْ يَحْيَى بْنِ وَثَّابٍ، عَنِ ابْنِ عُمَرَ، عَنِ النَّبِيِّ صلى الله عليه وسلم قَالَ: الْمُؤْمِنُ الَّذِي يُخَالِطُ النَّاسَ، وَيَصْبِرُ عَلَى أَذَاهُمْ، خَيْرٌ مِنَ الَّذِي لاَ يُخَالِطُ النَّاسَ، وَلاَ يَصْبِرُ عَلَى أَذَاهُمْ.
(البخاري في الادب المفرد)

Ibn 'Umar (RA) reported that the Prophet, may Allah bless him and grant him peace, said: 'The believer who mixes with people and endures their harm is better than the person who does not mix with people nor endures their harm.' (Bukhārī in *al-Adab al-Mufrad*)

COMMENTARY

Community workers shall not be surprised by the trouble they may face from the same people they are trying to serve. After all, this was the case with several prophets, such as

Prophet Mūsā, may Allah send him peace, who struggled with the continuous complains of his companions:

> **They said, 'We have been harmed before you came to us and after you have come to us.' He said, 'Perhaps your Lord will destroy your enemy and grant you succession in the land and see how you will do.'** (al-Aʿrāf 7: 129)

In the case of community activism, this harm could be manifested in accusations made against its leaders. Other times, it could be pointless debates and arguments within the internal team that result in division and disunity (there is more on this in hadith 32). The pressure from dealing with a dysfunctional group may push many activists to shield themselves from all the potential trouble. This tendency is exacerbated once we add to it the individualism that influences different aspects of the modern world: the excessive emphasis on *I* versus *we*, and the focus on self-actualization and selfish goals, as opposed to communal endeavours and aspirations. For all these reasons, the hadith at hand is a major element of every educational program for activists and community workers.

In Islamic tradition, the discussion on seclusion references hadith about the end of times, where specific guidance is given to preserve one's identity and faith during trials and tribulations. An example is a lengthy advice to Ḥudhayfah ibn al-Yamān (RA), which was concluded by Ḥudhayfah asking:

> *'What if I could not find a congregation and be a leader to the believers?', and Prophet Muhammad, may Allah bless him and give him peace, answered by saying: 'Then turn away from all these sects and seclude yourself, even if your only source of food is to gnaw on the roots of a tree until death comes for you!'* (Bukhārī and Muslim)

Without any ambiguity, all of these hadith reference the deterioration in people's faith and commitment to Islamic principles, and the ever-increasing amount of personal and communal trials. However, this valuable prophetic advice should not be used to justify seclusion away from righteous company and friends. Unfortunately, this is very common amongst believers and activists who get burned out from community work, and try to run away from the clashes and internal conflicts that happen within a Muslim organization. Why is this problematic? Because those people do not become completely secluded from society as a whole, as the hadith suggests. They will still be influenced by their family, social and professional circles, and the media. At this point, such an incomplete understanding of the hadith on seclusion becomes extremely worrisome, since the main objective is the preservation of faith and Muslim identity. Ibn Ḥajar (RA) emphasizes this in his commentary by saying: 'This narration indicates the virtue of seclusion specifically for those who are afraid of losing their religion and their identity.'

ACTION ITEMS

1. This hadith does not invite us to be passively patient with people's harmfulness or mistakes. As guided by other hadith and Qur'anic verses, a Muslim is expected to be proactive in cases of conflict between other co-workers and volunteers, as in the story of Prophets Musa and Harun in *Ṭa-Ha* 20: 94, may Allah send them peace. Our brotherhood and sisterhood necessitate that we clear our hearts of any misgivings and not leave any unanswered misconceptions or unresolved issues. Otherwise, hatred, jealousy and backbiting will spread amongst the hearts and the Devil will easily manipulate these feelings to remove the *barakah* from an organization's efforts.

   If someone is uncomfortable with confrontation, they can defer the discussion to wait for the right moment or seek the help of more experienced members or mentors. However, they should not completely ignore such emotions for the sake of superficial unity with the excuse of being patient. In addition to patience, we need honest and sincere advice (hadith 8) as well as holding a good opinion of others' intentions if we really want our community endeavours to be fruitful.

2. Ibn al-Jawzī (RA) in a famous statement criticized the monks for secluding themselves from the people, even if it was meant to attain higher levels of spirituality:

The monks are behaving like bats in their caves: they have buried themselves by not benefiting others. Such seclusion might be good provided that other acts of goodness are maintained such as congregational prayer, attending a funeral, or visiting the sick; however, even then seclusion will be the choice of the coward. As for the courageous, they keep learning and teaching everyday (by interacting with people), and such is the status of the Prophets (peace be upon them).[27]

3. In some specific cases, temporary solitude may be a necessary solution for community activists. This could be for family reasons, spiritual rejuvenation, or to take a break for mental wellbeing. However, such people should not ignore the impact of righteous companions and friends, and should ensure that they are connected to such environments even during their hiatus.

HADITH 22
APPRECIATE EACH TALENT

عَنْ مُحَمَّدِ بْنِ عَبْدِ اللَّهِ بْنِ زَيْدٍ، عَنْ أَبِيهِ، قَالَ لَمَّا أَصْبَحْنَا أَتَيْنَا رَسُولَ اللَّهِ صلى الله عليه وسلم فَأَخْبَرْتُهُ بِالرُّؤْيَا فَقَالَ ' إِنَّ هَذِهِ لَرُؤْيَا حَقٌّ فَقُمْ مَعَ بِلاَلٍ فَإِنَّهُ أَنْدَى وَأَمَدُّ صَوْتًا مِنْكَ فَأَلْقِ عَلَيْهِ مَا قِيلَ لَكَ وَلْيُنَادِ بِذَلِكَ '
(الترمذي)

27 Ibn al-Jawzī, *Ṣa'yd al-Khāṭir*.

ʿAbdullāh ibn Zayd (RA) narrated: 'After I had a dream (of the adhān*), I went to the Messenger of Allah, may Allah bless him and give him peace, in the morning to tell him about it. He said, "Indeed this dream is true. So go to Bilāl, for he has a better and louder voice than you, and recite to him what was given to you, so that he may call to the prayer with it.'"* (Tirmidhī)

COMMENTARY

The background of this hadith goes back to the early days of Madinah, when the newly-formed Muslim community was brainstorming ways to call people to prayer. The Messenger of Allah, may Allah bless him and give him peace, did not receive any direct revelation on this, as had been the case with multiple acts of worship.[28] This motivated the Companions to give different suggestions, such as the Christian way (ringing bells) or the Jewish way (blowing a horn), but they did not reach any conclusion at the first meeting. The narrator of this hadith, ʿAbdullāh ibn Zayd (RA), saw in his dream that night an angel reciting the words of the *adhān* as we know it now. At dawn, he rushed to the *masjid* to narrate his dream. The Prophet Muhammad, may Allah bless him and give him peace, approved of the dream's message and recognized

28 The books of *Fiqh* define the Sunnah as the actions and speeches of the messenger (may Allah bless him and give him peace) in addition to the times where he approved the actions of others. This latter category includes incidents such as the legislation of the *adhān*, where it became a valid Sunnah due to the approval of Prophet Muhammad to the dream that was seen by ʿAbdullāh ibn Zayd as well as ʿUmar ibn al-Khaṭṭāb.

ʿAbdullāh's contribution. However, he assigned the task of calling the *adhān* to Bilāl ibn Rabāḥ (RA). The criterion for selecting Bilāl were stated clearly—he had a better voice, one that was stronger, louder and simply more beautiful.

Beyond the legal (*fiqh*) implications of this hadith, it has a lot of implications for community leaders. It shows that when someone starts a new project, he or she is encouraged to seek out the right talent to execute it. Instead of disputing about who should own or lead the project, the focus should be on achieving the goal with the best outcome. In community affairs, the cause is always bigger than the individual, and no one shall assume any exclusive rights as the originator of an idea, as the founder of an organisation, or as the funder of a project. In fact, the true impact of a project can only be realized when those outside the founding team adopt it and treat it as their own.

The Prophet's recognition and appreciation of the diverse talents of his Companions was manifested in other hadith. Anas ibn Mālik (RA) narrated that the Messenger of Allah, may Allah bless him and give him peace, said,

> *The most merciful of my* ummah *towards my* ummah *is Abū Bakr; the one who adheres most sternly to the religion of Allah is ʿUmar; the most sincere of them in shyness and modesty is ʿUthmān; the best judge is ʿAlī ibn Abī Ṭālib; the best in reciting the Book of Allah is Ubayy ibn Kaʿb; the most knowledgeable of what is lawful and unlawful is Muʿādh ibn Jabal; and the most knowledgeable of the rules of inheritance* (farā'iḍ) *is Zayd ibn Thābit. And every nation*

has a trustworthy guardian, and the trustworthy guardian of this ummah *is Abū 'Ubaydah ibn al-Jarrāḥ.* (Tirmidhi)

ACTION ITEMS

1. This hadith suggests that nobody should own an idea, a project, a committee, or a line of work and claim it to be theirs. Sometimes community activists, despite being sincere, may become emotionally invested in a cause and refuse to give it away. They cannot imagine anyone else handling such position or contributing to it. Unfortunately, those around them may feed such misperceptions of self-importance, ownership, and exclusive rights. Clearly, we should thank such people for their sacrifice and initiation of every noble project, but at the same time advise them that successful work should always outgrow its founders. Our community has to shift its mindset from a focus on leaders, heroes, and celebrities towards building institutions.

2. Self-awareness is an important trait for all of those who are trying to make a difference in this world. Encourage your team to understand how they fit into the fabric of your organization, to the Muslim community, and to the world at large. Help them in assessing their strengths, recognising their weaknesses, and to appreciate what makes them unique compared with others. Recently, multiple

forms of personality tests, such has the Myers-Briggs test, have surfaced as a quick fix towards identifying an individual personality, even when such tests are not based on authentic scientific research.[29] While it is true that there are some ways to identify one's strengths based on their previous experience,[30] such approaches may be viewed as a starting point rather than being an objective assessment. Moreover, activists should constantly work on increasing their self-awareness through reflecting on the Qur'an, seclusion (*I'tikāf*), reading biographies of leaders and influential figures, experimenting with different roles within the community, all that in addition to seeking advice and mentorship.

In any event, one should realize the complicated and evolving nature of the human personality, and hence the limitations of such assessments. It is advised that activists use valid assessment methods only as a starting point, while investing time and effort in self-awareness and self-development.[31]

29 Hardy, B, *Personality Isn't Permanent, Break Free From Self-Limiting Beliefs and Rewrite Your Story*(Penguin Random House, 2020).

30 Rath, T, *StrengthsFinder 2.0* (Simon and Schuster, 2007).

31 Usman, O., August 4, 2016, 'Why Bad Leaders Rise to the Top, And Why We Keep Following Them' https://medium.com/@ibnabeeomar/why-bad-leaders-rise-to-the-top-and-why-we-keep-following-them-22125c30c91b, last accessed December 2021.

3. This hadith invites the leadership of Muslim organisations to set the right expectations on hiring and evaluating community leaders, teachers, imams and organizers. Instead of setting high expectations of an all-rounder, polymath, or Renaissance man who is a jack-of-all-trades, we need to be realistic in our approach. Your group should get into the habit of writing clear job descriptions with well-defined requirements of the necessary skills and the expectations. Moreover, we should seek subject matter experts in areas that are essential for our community. In addition to deep and authentic Islamic knowledge, we need to seek experts in strategic planning, conflict resolution, management, operations management, facilities maintenance, bookkeeping and accounting, event planning, fundraising, project management, construction, educational administration, and the list goes on.

HADITH 23
RIGHTS AND RESPONSIBILITIES OF LEADERS

عن أبي هريرة رضي الله عنه قال: قال رسول الله صلى الله عليه وسلم 'عليك السمع والطاعة في عسرك ويسرك ومنشطك، ومكرهك وأثرة عليك' (رواه مسلم).

Abū Hurayrah, may Allah be pleased with him, reported that the Messenger of Allah, may Allah bless him and give him peace, said: 'It is mandatory upon you to follow the commands

> *of those in charge at times of prosperity or adversity, whether you are motivated or not, and whether you feel someone was given preference over you or not.'* (Muslim)

COMMENTARY

Islam calls for establishing the right framework for a healthy relationship between a leader and the rest of the team. Without it, the group will have a tendency towards one of two extremes: authoritarian leaders who expect blind following without any questions, or haphazard or uncommitted leadership that can produce undisciplined members with wishy-washy commitment to the organization's structure and chain of command. The first rule in Islam is that of obedience and trust to the leader, so long as their commands do not contradict with the teachings of the Qur'an and the Sunnah: *'No human is to be obeyed in matters of disobedience to Allah, for obedience shall only be in matters of righteousness.'* (Bukhārī and Muslim)

Once we ensure that the commands given are aligned with Islamic principles, we should realize that our obedience to our teachers, mentors, and leaders can be considered an act of worship to Allah Almighty:

> **O you who have believed, obey Allah and obey the Messenger and those in authority among you. And if you disagree over anything, refer it to Allah and the Messenger, if you should believe in Allah and the Last Day.** (al-Nisā' 4: 59)

The discussion on discipline and obedience is so important in our day and age, especially if we consider the rise of individualism and the tendency to reject any type of authority. Such trends can easily find their way into Muslim organizations, and cause a divide between community members, especially when volunteers from multiple backgrounds and generations are trying to work together. In addition, it goes without saying that discipline and compliance to commands may seem effortless if the direction of the organization is in line with my preferences. The real test, however, is when I feel neutral or even in disagreement about the decisions made: I will not be motivated to follow through! But this is where the true test of faith and humility comes, in supporting and even adopting the position of my leadership as though it is my own!

On the other hand, leaders have a bigger responsibility to earn the trust of their teams by fulfilling the duty of consultation:

> **And those who responded to their Lord; keep up the prayer; conduct their affairs by mutual consultation.** (al-Shūrā 42: 38)

The Prophet Muhammad, may Allah bless him and give him peace, showed the best examples of *shūrā* on multiple occasions during his life. Before the Battle of Badr, he responded to the suggestion from al-Habbāb ibn al-Mundhir (RA) to move the whole Muslim army in front of the Well of Badr. The same happened during the Battle of the Trench, when Salmān al-Fārisī (RA) proposed the idea of digging the trench to protect Madinah. Even at times when the outcome of such consultation resulted in a defeat for the Muslims, the Qur'an encouraged the Messenger (may Allah bless him and send him peace) to keep up the practice of consultation.

An example of this was the battle of Uḥud, when the Prophet, may Allah bless him and give him peace, agreed to leave Madinah and fight the Quraysh outside its boundaries, which was not his initial plan. Clearly, when the Muslim army were defeated, one would expect some voices within the community to blame the practice of consultation itself: that the youth among the Companions should have listened to the Messenger's initial advice and stayed in Madinah. However, Allah commended His Messenger, may Allah bless him and give him peace, for practising *shūrā*, and praised him for showing mercy and gentleness towards the Companions:

> **By an act of mercy from God, you [Prophet] were gentle in your dealings with them—had you been harsh, or hard-hearted, they would have dispersed and left you—so pardon them and ask forgiveness for them. Consult with them about matters, then, when you have decided on a course of action, put your trust in God: God loves those who put their trust in Him.** (Āl ʿImrān 3: 159)

FURTHER DISCUSSION ON RIGHTS AND RESPONSIBILITIES OF LEADERS IN ISLAM

1. Some volunteers and community members may question the necessity of having a leader. This is in order to avoid conflicts and power struggles. Some people may be inclined to the notion of being casual activists, as part of a group of friends who just want to help out without anyone being really in charge. Clearly, this reasoning and approach is flawed if those volunteers want to have a sustainable impact on the cause they care about. Moreover, such a way of thinking contradicts clear prophetic direction on the necessity of having a leader (*amīr*):

   Abū Sa'īd al-Khudrī and Abū Hurayrah, may Allah be pleased with them, reported that the Messenger of Allah, may Allah bless him and give him peace, said, 'When three people set out on a journey, they should appoint one among themselves as their leader.' (Abū Dāwūd)

   Ibn Taymiyyah, may Allah have mercy on him, comments on this beautifully by remarking:

   As the Messenger of Allah, may Allah bless him and give him peace, has ordained the appointment of a leader (*imārah*) in the smallest of gatherings, such as of three people, and in ephemeral situations, like travelling, this highlights the obligation of doing so for gatherings and durations that extend beyond that.

2. Muslim teams who would like to tap into the spiritual blessings (*barakah*) from Allah should genuinely establish *shūrā* among themselves. It is a matter of fulfilling a Divine duty first, and then an issue of trying to invite and encourage differing opinions and viewpoints. Al-Ḥasan once said, 'People never seek advice without being guided to the best possibility available to them.' He then recited the verse: **And they manage their affairs by mutual consultation.'** (al-Shūrā 42: 38) (Bukhārī, *Kitāb al-Adab al-Mufrad*)

3. Establish with your team clear ways to incorporate *shūrā* into the governance of your non-profit organization, while keeping in mind the following key principles:

    - *Shūrā* is limited to decisions that are permissible in Islam, as there is no *shūrā* permitted to contravene rulings that are well established in Islamic law. The value system of a Muslim organization shall not be subject to the preferences of its members, as, by definition, they have to affirm the rules and regulations that are set by Allah Almighty.

    - The essence of *shūrā* does not align perfectly with counting the votes of the majority, which favours superficial factors, such as one's popularity, connections or outspokenness. In spirit, *shūrā* calls for giving each side enough time to be fully discussed and considered. However, once duly considered, the majority of the votes of trusted committee members (please see the following point below) may be considered decisive, so long as it is based on a well-informed basis.

- According to Islamic principles, a *shūrā* committee has to include trustworthy individuals—commonly referred to as the ones who can secure and loosen the bonds and ties (*ahl al-ḥall wa'l-'aqd*). As al-Juwaynī elaborates, 'These are the independent and righteous individuals who have been shaped by experience. They have seen multiple paths and options and identified the important traits of the one who should be in charge of leading the masses.'[32]

32 Al-Juwaynī, *al-Ghayāthī*.

CHAPTER 5

THE HOW [1]

THE ADAB OF ACTIVISM

ISLAM IS NOT a cultural or ethnic identity, but a complete value system and way of life that is inspired by Divine revelation. Muslim activists cannot claim to carry the banner of Islam and work for a Muslim cause without at least striving to live Islam and fulfil its commands in a holistic manner: **You who believe, enter wholeheartedly into submission to God and do not follow in Satan's footsteps, for he is your sworn enemy.** (al-Baqarah 2: 208)

One of the main objectives of the message of Islam is to instil manners and good character (*adab*) into the believers. The Messenger of Allah, peace and blessings be upon him, said: '*I have been sent to perfect good character.*' (Mālik)

The Qur'an emphasizes how the acts of worship in Islam should affect our character and manners:

- The five daily prayers: **Establish the prayer: for prayer restrains the believers from outrageous and unacceptable behaviour.** (al-'Ankabūt 29: 45)

- Charity: **In order to cleanse and purify them (Prophet), accept a gift out of their property (to make amends).** (al-Tawbah 9: 103)

- Fasting: **Believers, fasting is prescribed for you, as it was prescribed for those before you, so that you may be mindful of God.** (al-Baqarah 2: 183)

- Hajj: **There should be no indecent speech, misbehaviour or quarrelling for anyone undertaking the pilgrimage.** (al-Baqarah 2: 197)

The following chapter highlights only a few selected hadith that are important for activists and community workers to keep in mind. The reader is referred to original compilations such as *Riyāḍ al-Ṣāliḥīn* for a more exhaustive selection of hadith on manners and character.[33]

33 Imam Nawawī – *Riyāḍ al-Ṣāliḥīn*.

HADITH 24
SINCERE GOODWILL

عَنْ أَبِي رُقَيَّةَ تَمِيمِ بْنِ أَوْسٍ الدَّارِيِّ رَضِيَ اللهُ عَنْهُ أَنَّ النَّبِيَّ صلى الله عليه وسلم قَالَ: 'الدِّينُ النَّصِيحَةُ.' قُلْنَا: لِمَنْ؟ قَالَ: 'لِلَّهِ، وَلِكِتَابِهِ، وَلِرَسُولِهِ، وَلِأَئِمَّةِ الْمُسْلِمِينَ وَعَامَّتِهِمْ.' (رواه مسلم)

Tamīm al-Dārī reported that the Messenger of Allah, may Allah bless him and give him peace, said: 'The religion is all about sincere goodwill (naṣīḥah).' We said: 'To whom?' The Prophet said, 'To Allah, His book, His Messenger, the leaders of the Muslims and their common people.' (Muslim)

COMMENTARY

The discussion on activism invites us to consider the bigger picture of the Islamic ethical system, particularly the concept of *naṣīḥah*. One can think of this word as the epitome of sincerity, purity, and advice, both in terms of giving and receiving sincere goodwill. The root Arabic word for *naṣīḥah* is *naṣaḥa*, which refers to purifying something, cleansing from it any deceit, and freeing it from all flaws. It is interesting to note that the Arabs associated the act of giving advice to being honest, sincere, and straightforward. It was never about public shaming and call-out culture, but a sincere care for the other person before, during, and after delivering the advice. In the Qur'an, we see this genuine love and care in the speech that Prophet Saleh gave to his community:

> **And he turned away from them and said, 'O my people, I had certainly conveyed to you the message of my Lord and advised you (naṣahtu lakum), but you do not like advisors.'** (al-Aʿrāf 7: 79)

After realizing the different dimensions of the word *naṣīḥah*, one can examine how it applies to the remainder of the hadith:

> *Naṣīḥah* in respect of *Allah* means absolute sincerity and devotion to Him, and that a person establishes correct relations with Allah, His commands, and His warnings.
>
> *Naṣīḥah* in respect of the *Prophet* is to accept him as the supreme guide, leader, and the walking example of the Qur'an.
>
> *Naṣīḥah* in respect of the *leaders of Muslim society and common folk* is to give them good advice, enjoin the good and forbid the evil, and speak truth to power (see hadith 13).

In addition to sincerity and good manners, the Qur'an provides some details on the *fiqh* of *naṣīḥah*:

> **(Prophet), call (people) to the way of your Lord with wisdom and good teaching. Argue with them in the most courteous way.** (al-Naḥl 16: 125)

Al-Saʿdī comments on this *āyah* by saying:

> Use wisdom (*ḥikmah*) with all persons (believers and nonbelievers) when you invite them to the path of Allah and beneficial knowledge and righteous deeds. Wisdom is that you address each person based on their situation, understanding, and adherence to submission. It ensures that such preaching is based on knowledge not ignorance, and starts with the most important matters first, and with commands that are more likely to be accepted, using the gentlest and kindest words.[34]

If the person does not respond, then the next level is excellence in warning (*al-mawʿiẓah al-ḥasanah*), which entails reminding the person about the consequences of their actions and using words of encouragement as well as words of warning. One could mention the benefits of responding to the commands of Allah, and the harmful effects of disobedience. Now if the person being counselled insists that what they follow is the truth, or is a promoter of falsehood, then the next step is to debate with them in the most courteous manner and reason, and employ the most convincing arguments using both revelation as well as logical arguments.

34 *Tafsīr al-Saʿdī.*

ACTION ITEMS

1. Muslim activists should check their intention before giving someone *naṣīḥah*: are we sincere in trying to help a brother to get better? Or is the intention to insult others and show off our knowledge and our superiority? Did we make *du'ā'* so that Allah helps us choose the best words, and help the sinner improve due to our words, as told in 20: 25–35? The act of giving advice should stem from our hearts and should be an opportunity for more humility and self-awareness, not the other way around.

2. Receiving advice and critique is as important as, if not more so, than giving it. Community organizers should establish regular forums and venues for open lines of communication and advice. A man once disagreed with 'Umar ibn al-Khaṭṭāb and advised him to fear Allah! People started rebuking the man for disrespecting the leader of the believers. 'Umar, may Allah be pleased with him, replied, 'Leave him, for there is nothing good left in the people if they don't say it to us, and there is nothing good left in us if it is not said to us.'[35]

3. In another hadith narrated by Imam al-Bukhārī, the Prophet Muhammad, may Allah bless him and

35 Abu Zayd Al-Basri, *The History of Al-Madinah Al-Munawwarah*. It is worth noting that many scholars question the authenticity of this incident. Still, its moral theme is aligned with 'Umar's leadership style and firmness with himself and others.

give him peace, described a believer as a 'mirror' to other believers. The imagery used in this hadith to describe *naṣīḥah* between the believers can be used as an inspiration for a team-building activity: team members can reflect on the analogy between giving advice and checking one's self using a mirror. While there might be unlimited benefits from this hadith, here are some starting thoughts:

a. A mirror reveals all the flaws of the person looking at it and does not hide anything.

b. A mirror gives advice about one's appearance in private and when asked.

c. A mirror's advice reflects light coming from an external light source, and similarly brotherly advice should also stem from the source of revelation and light (the Qur'an and the Sunnah)

4. It is important for us to realize the context of our *da'wah* and differentiate between different settings, for example, when counselling a person in private as compared to the issuing of a political statement. A weak person who may have slipped into a mistake is not the same as an open sinner who wants to spread corruption in society. This tells us that wisdom may require us to issue a *naṣīḥah* in public, call out a person by name, or use a harsh and firm tone depending on a situation.

HADITH 25
ETIQUETTE OF RECEIVING AND SHARING NEWS

عن أبي هريرة رضي الله عنه أن النبي صلى الله عليه وسلم قال: 'كفى بالمرء كذبًا أن يحدث بكل ما سمع'.(رواه مسلم)

Abū Hurayrah, may Allah be pleased with him, narrated that the Prophet, may Allah bless him and give him peace, said, 'It is enough for a man to prove himself a liar that he narrates whatever he hears.' (Muslim)

COMMENTARY

This hadith established a mindset amongst Muslim scholars that helped preserve and spread authentic Islamic sciences. The main teachings of Islam have reached us after many centuries through strong chains of narration that have withstood the test of time alongside political and theological differences. This could not have happened had the scholars not applied this mindset to establish processes that verified every narration that we have received. Basically, they started with the assumption that every narration is inaccurate unless proven otherwise. 'Abdullah ibn al-Mubarak once said: 'Verifying narrators (*isnad*) is a major part of our religion, and had it not been there, then anyone could have said anything in Islam.'[36]

36 Imam Nawawī's explanation of *Ṣaḥīḥ Muslim*.

In activism and community work, Muslims should extend this mindset and adopt it in all aspects of their communal life and work. The Qur'an teaches us to verify any news that reaches us before we make a judgement and rush to make any response:

> **O you who have believed, if there comes to you a disobedient one with information, investigate, lest you harm a people out of ignorance and become, over what you have done, regretful.** (al-Ḥujurāt 49: 6)

Another dimension that this hadith teaches is to simply remain silent unless there is something good and valuable to share. Believers should resist the urge to immediately share whatever they receive or hear, even when the intention is good, to warn people or raise awareness. We should ask ourselves; (i) is the information valid; (ii) is it useful to share; and (iii) who should hear or not hear this information. The human tendency to be the first to report or broadcast has been exacerbated in the age of online media and news outlets; metrics and incentives in the digital age have become only about how much attention and how many clicks and visits are being attracted, with little to no emphasis on value or validity. The Qur'an warns from having some of the traits of the hypocrites:

> **If any matter comes to them concerning security or fear, they spread it around. But if they had only referred it to the Messenger or to those charged with authority, those among them who are able to investigate and think out the matter would indeed know (what to do with) it.** (al-Nisā' 4: 83)

This *āyah* encourages the believers to refer sensitive information to their leadership or to the Messenger, may Allah bless him and give him peace. The leaders' calmness, wisdom and sound judgement are of critical importance in choosing how to react in such circumstances. They are expected to do their due diligence and assess the reaction of the public, especially in times of turmoil when emotions are high. Hadith 28 reiterates the same message more concisely: *a believer in Allah and the last day should either speak good or remain silent.*

ACTION ITEMS

1. Verify every piece of information you receive about other believers and community members. By applying this hadith, a lot of harm, gossip and ill-intent can be mitigated, and the community can be saved from divisions that might result from unverified assumptions and news. Try to go straight to the original source of the rumour and ask, 'Is it true that you said such and such?' There is no need to beat around the bush and complicate the process of fact-checking with community members if we all truly wish to please Allah, glorified and exalted is He, and keep our hearts pure.

2. Train your team and your volunteers on how to read and verify the news that we receive. Whether it comes to complicated issues involving international politics or to relationships between different

organizations, the basics of media literacy should not change: for example, how to break down an article, distinguish an opinion piece from a news piece, and identify sources and fact-check them.

3. Cut down on information consumption, reflect deeply and internalize the news you receive, and try to diversify your sources of knowledge. Try to follow and check websites and individuals that you completely disagree with and cross check with how they view and perceive things.[37]

4. When Abū Bakr received the news of the Night Journey (*al-Isrā'*) on behalf of the Messenger, may Allah bless him and give him peace, he commented by saying, 'If he said so, then he has definitely spoken the truth.'[38] His love for the Messenger did not blind him from keeping in mind that the news report, which seemed unbelievable, could have been fabricated. After this incident, Abū Bakr was given the honorific: 'Al-Ṣiddīq', the one who truly believes the Messenger of Allah, may Allah bless him and give him peace. This connects two elements together: (i) unshakable belief in Islam and

37 Usman, O. November 23, 2016, Trump's Master Class In Media Manipulation, False News, And The Hadith That Predicted It All, [website], https://www.ibnabeeomar.com/blog/trumps-master-class-media-manipulation-false-news-hadith-predicted-fiqhofsocialmedia, last accessed December 2021.

38 Narrated by al-Ḥākim.

(ii) awareness of the possibility of misinformation and misrepresentation. Without such deliberate practice, activists could easily lose their credibility and hurt the same causes that they care about.

HADITH 26
EXCELLENCE: THE DNA OF A MUSLIM'S WORK

عَنْ أَبِي يَعْلَى شَدَّادِ بْنِ أَوْسٍ رَضِيَ اللهُ عَنْهُ عَنْ رَسُولِ اللَّهِ صلى الله عليه و سلم قَالَ: 'إنَّ اللَّهَ كَتَبَ الْإِحْسَانَ عَلَى كُلِّ شَيْءٍ، فَإِذَا قَتَلْتُمْ فَأَحْسِنُوا الْقِتْلَةَ، وَإِذَا ذَبَحْتُمْ فَأَحْسِنُوا الذِّبْحَةَ، وَلْيُحِدَّ أَحَدُكُمْ شَفْرَتَهُ، وَلْيُرِحْ ذَبِيحَتَهُ'. (رَوَاهُ مُسْلِمٌ)

Shaddād ibn Aws (RA) reported that the Messenger of Allah, peace and blessings be upon him, said: 'Verily, Allah has prescribed excellence in everything. If you have to kill, then kill in the least painful manner. And if you have to slaughter, then slaughter in the best possible way. Let one of you sharpen his knife so his animal is spared any suffering.' (Muslim)

COMMENTARY

Excellence (*iḥsān*) is an inherent trait that Allah the Creator has given to His servants, when He perfected their creation:

He is the one Who perfected everything which He created. (Luqmān 32: 7)

And in return, Allah the Almighty expects the same attitude from us: to pursue excellence in our worship and service towards Him and then towards His creation:

> **(He) who created death and life to test you (as to) which of you is best in deeds.** (al-Mulk 67: 2)

And due to His ultimate mercy and generosity, He promised to reward our little and incomplete efforts of *iḥsān* with His infinitely vast reward of *iḥsān* in the Hereafter:

> **Those who did well will have the best reward and more besides. Neither darkness nor shame will cover their faces: these are the companions in Paradise, and there they will remain.** (Yūnus 10: 26)

In the hadith at hand, the Prophet, may Allah bless him and give him peace, invites us to extend our *iḥsān* to details that we may overlook or deem unnecessary. Even when slaughtering an animal, we should pursue excellence in the process and the tools used, and, according to some scholars, make sure that other animals don't see the animal being killed. The essence of *iḥsān* is when you do not expect anything in return (whether it is a compliment or a complaint). The essence of *iḥsān* is to be mindful that you are dealing with Allah in all of your affairs, not with the human, animal, plant, or inanimate object that you are tending to:

> *'Excellence is to worship Allah as if you see Him, for if you do not see Him, He surely sees you.'* (Muslim)

In another sound hadith, Prophet Muhammad, may Allah bless him and give him peace, enforced the message of *iḥsān* even when performing a task that will not be seen by anyone:

> *ʿĀṣim narrates that his father witnessed a funeral where the Prophet Muhammad, may Allah bless him and give him peace, commanded the people to fix the inside of the grave. He started giving detailed instructions to the one digging the grave until the people assumed that such instructions were a Sunnah. The Prophet, may Allah bless him and give him peace, commented: 'Indeed, this does not bring any benefit or harm to the deceased, but indeed Allah loves that when one of you performs a deed that he completes it with excellence.'* (Bayhaqī)

ACTION ITEMS

1. The *Iḥsān* mindset for Muslim activists should help us realize that in every event or community project, we are dealing with Allah first, before dealing with any audience, organization, or colleagues. This shifts our attention from quantity to quality, from counting the number of followers to establishing deeper and meaningful relationships. Such *iḥsān* can only be attained if we establish it first in our worship, for example in our daily prayers, and then allow it to trickle down to other aspects of our lives—our career, school, relationships, marriage, parenting, for example.

2. A Muslim activist with the *iḥsān* mindset does not behave differently whether the work for the community is volunteer-based or compensated. Some people assume that because such work is unpaid that it is okay to be mediocre and so they don't give such work their best attention. They may justify such an attitude by being overcommitted to multiple projects, which results in reducing the care and attention they can give to a particular commitment. However, this hadith and many others encourage us to reduce the number of tasks that we take on, while raising the bar in excelling in the service that we are providing. We should prioritize and care for what Allah loves (*iḥsān* in our work) as opposed to the fake illusion of 'spreading more good work' which may or may not have a long-lasting impact.

3. *Iḥsān* shifts our attention from metrics that are beyond our control, such as winning an election, raising funds, or improving the behaviour of a student. Such metrics are considered 'lag measures'[39] as they happen late in or after the process, and they also involve other people's behaviour. Instead, *iḥsān* leads us to focus on 'lead' measures, on specific actions that we can control and influence. We can establish an '*iḥsān* score card' to monitor spiritual elements, such as making *du'ā'* and renewing

39 Newport, C., *Deep work : rules for focused success in a distracted world,* (New York : Grand Central Publishing, 2016).

intentions, as well as implementation-oriented ones, such as the cleanliness of the venue, the number of hours spent in preparation, in addition to timeliness in execution.

4. Recite and reflect with your team on the beautiful story of Prophet Sulaymān (RA), and how every member of his community practiced *iḥsān* in what they did (*al-Naml* 27: 15-44). From the ants and the birds to the soldiers and the scholars, the value of *iḥsān* in his kingdom was at a different level. All that led to the result of impressing the Queen of Sheba who eventually accepted Islam.

HADITH 27
THE ONE BODY

عن أبي موسى رضي الله عنه قال: قال رسول الله صلى الله عليه وسلم ' المؤمن للمؤمن كالبنيان يشد بعضه بعضًا' وشبك بين أصابعه . (متفق عليه) .

Abū Mūsā, may Allah be pleased with him, reported that the Messenger of Allah, may Allah bless him and give him peace, said: 'The believers' relationship to one another is like that of bricks in the same building, each one strengthens and supports the other.' The Prophet illustrated this by interlacing the fingers of both his hands. (Bukhārī and Muslim)

COMMENTARY

This is another hadith, like hadith 9 and 11, that uses beautiful imagery to deliver the prophetic message. This prophetic educational method summarizes hours of preaching by presenting a concrete example that sticks in people's minds.[40] It converts abstract teachings of the *dīn* into tangible objects around us and helps us to understand and practise Islam to our everyday lives. In terms of brotherhood and unity of the Muslim *ummah*, the Prophet, may Allah bless him and give him peace, used two examples:

Believers are like building blocks within the same structure: these bricks uniformly carry the weight of a building. They maintain synergy in between each other while working for the same goal. They understand that their value only comes when they are united, otherwise they would be fragmented pieces that are worthless. They do not compete, because each brick among them has a well-defined position and value. They know that if one of them were to get loose or break, then the whole structure would be put in danger, for the contribution of each member is critical to the success of the community.

Believers as organs in the same human body: this one brings life into the believing community, and allows us to feel and hear the pulse inside the body of the *ummah*:

40 Sheikh Abdul-Fattah Abu Ghaddah, *Muhammad – The Perfect Teacher: An insight into his teaching methods.*

> *Al-Nuʿmān ibn Bashīr, may Allah be pleased with him, reported that the Messenger of Allah, may Allah bless him and give him peace, said: 'The believers in their mutual kindness, compassion and sympathy are just like one body. When one of the limbs suffers, the whole body responds to it with wakefulness and fever.'* (Bukhārī and Muslim)

One of the unfortunate outcomes of modernity is the inflation of the ego and self-actualization at the expense of communal and societal harmony. Even when it comes to charity and non-profit work, the quest to leave a legacy and to have an impact have become individualistic endeavours. Islam is not against the principle, so long as we start such legacies to benefit the whole community with Allah's pleasure in mind and heart. Without cultivating such an attitude, different organizations may develop an unhealthy sense of competition, and forget the simple fact that all are supposed to be serving the same cause. Competition in and of itself is not problematic, and it is in fact encouraged in the Qur'an to compete for the highest level of Paradise: **And in aspiring for this, the competitors should compete.** (al-Muṭaffifīn 83: 26) However, it is problematic when different groups develop a scarcity mindset, and consider the success of another to be taking away from their own, when they consider that the amount of donations raised or the attendance at events to be a zero-sum game, and lose sight of the bigger picture: that no single organization or teacher or relief group can completely fulfil all the duties or obligations. All Muslim groups have one united cause to save the ship of humanity (as in hadith 11), and all of them belong to the same body and the same structure.

ACTION ITEMS

1. Ensure that your events and organizations provide equal awareness and support for the diverse causes that the Muslim *ummah* is suffering from around the world. It is understandable that your community may feel inclined towards a particular country or cause. After all, Islam does not necessitate that the believers forget or ignore their cultural background, as long as it does not create tribal divisions and racism. However, Muslim leaders and activists should not be completely oblivious to the struggles of other Muslims. This can be mitigated by (i) education; (ii) building bridges with other communities; and (iii) approaching each cause with empathy and care. Moreover, we should consider the big picture and connect the dots on how different social justice causes are related. More on this topic is presented below in hadith 32. This care for one another and the one-body mindset should be reflected in mentioning all the oppressed communities in our supplication, such as during the Friday prayer, or at least to be generic in our wording.

2. Our care for the Muslim *ummah* should not turn us into pessimistic spectators whose only job is to follow the painful news of the suffering of Muslims worldwide. There is a weak hadith that is often quoted in this regard, 'He who does not care about the affairs of the Muslims is not one of them.'[41]

41 Rated as weak, according to al-Albānī.

Such weak hadith, despite having an apparently good meaning, should not be used to shame Muslim activists into following with desperation the sad news of Muslims across the world. There is a little nuance here, because the Prophet's message—if it were truly reported—was aimed at caring for the cause in a way that makes you educate yourself and others, and work to effectively change that reality. The aim is to turn your care and empathy into useful deeds that makes a difference on the immediate circles around you.

3. The Muslim *ummah* is one of the most diverse communities in ethnicity and race. The Qur'an encourages us to break the barriers between people and get to know one another. We should be intentional about establishing diversity in our communities, boards, events, meetings, etc. and not assume that it will happen by itself, especially when there is a dominant cultural background, such as all-Arab or all-Desi. Our organizations should value and celebrate such diversity and align themselves with the *ayah*:

   People, We created you all from a single man and a single woman, and made you into races and tribes so that you should recognize one another. In God's eyes, the most honoured of you are the ones most mindful of Him: God is all knowing, all aware. (al-Ḥujurāt 49: 13)

HADITH 28
IF YOU TRULY BELIEVE IN ALLAH AND THE LAST DAY

عَنْ أَبِي هُرَيْرَةَ رَضِيَ اللهُ عَنْهُ أَنَّ رَسُولَ اللَّهِ صلى الله عليه و سلم قَالَ: 'مَنْ كَانَ يُؤْمِنُ بِاَللَّهِ وَالْيَوْمِ الْآخِرِ فَلْيَقُلْ خَيْرًا أَوْ لِيَصْمُتْ، وَمَنْ كَانَ يُؤْمِنُ بِاَللَّهِ وَالْيَوْمِ الْآخِرِ فَلْيُكْرِمْ جَارَهُ، وَمَنْ كَانَ يُؤْمِنُ بِاَللَّهِ وَالْيَوْمِ الْآخِرِ فَلْيُكْرِمْ ضَيْفَهُ'.
(رَوَاهُ الْبُخَارِيُّ)

On the authority of Abū Hurayrah, may Allah be pleased with him, the Messenger of Allah, peace and blessings of Allah be upon him, said: 'Let him who believes in Allah and the Last Day speak good, or keep silent; and let him who believes in Allah and the Last Day be generous to his neighbour; and let him who believes in Allah and the Last Day be generous to his guest.' (Bukhārī and Muslim)

COMMENTARY

A Muslim's belief in Allah and the Day of Judgement should be reflected in their good manners towards all of Allah's creation. If this is true for every believer, then it is of particular importance to activists and community leaders who should lead by example and be role models to the ones they are trying to influence. Before worrying too much about the intellectual, organizational, and political dimensions of our activism, we should emphasize refining and improving our manners. By doing so, we are promised a high rank and proximity to our beloved Messenger, may Allah bless him and give him peace, in the Afterlife:

The dearest and the nearest to me among you on the Day of Resurrection are those who have the best manners; and the most hated among you, and those who will eventually be placed furthest from me on the Day of Judgement, are the ones who are the most talkative, the most pretentious, and the most arrogant. (Tirmidhī)

A. Speak Good or Remain Silent

Even when it comes to permissible speech, the Qur'an guides us to keep it limited and to avoid useless talk:

> **And those who turn away from idle or heedless talk.** (al-Mu'minūn 23: 3)

> *'Umar ibn al-Khaṭṭāb (RA) once said, 'If one's speech increases, his mistakes will also increase; when one's mistakes increase, his modesty will decrease; when one's modesty decreases, his piety will decrease; and when one's piety is decreased, his heart will die.'* (Ṭabarānī)

The hadith then suggests two great and noble deeds. Clearly, one cannot abstain from idle or evil talk without filling the otherwise wasted time with goodness.

B. Be Generous to Your Neighbour

The connection between faith and good manners is given greater emphasis when it comes to the rights of neighbours.

A person might be nice and friendly with strangers, or in the case of business transactions for the sake of mutual benefit. However, neighbours and family members are much closer to us, and maintaining good relations requires a higher level of discipline and good manners. This is why the least sign of faith, as mentioned in other narrations, is to refrain from inflicting any harm on one's neighbours. In another hadith, Abū Hurayrah, may Allah be pleased with him, narrated that the Prophet Muhammad, may Allah bless him and give him peace, was asked about a woman who prays during the night and fasts during the day, but had a sharp tongue that she used to malign her neighbours. He answered, '*There is no good in such woman, and she will be punished in the Hellfire.*' (al-Ḥākim)

C. Be Generous to Your Guest

To put things in context: for the Arabs, a guest was a traveller from another city or country with no place to stay or eat before there were institutions like hotels and restaurants. The cultural norm was to host a guest for three days. When hosting such people, the cultural norm also dictated that the host only ask them about their whereabouts and plans after the third day. We see such hospitality in the story of Ibrahim with the angels who visited him in the form of travelling men:

> **Have you heard the story of the honoured guests of Abraham? They went in to see him and said, 'Peace'. 'Peace,' he said, adding to himself: 'These people are strangers.' He turned quickly to his household,**

> **brought out a fat calf, and placed it near them; he said, 'Will you not eat?' And he felt from them apprehension. They said, 'Fear not,' and gave him good tidings of a learned boy.** (al-Dhāriyāt 51: 24-28)

'Abdullāh ibn 'Amr (RA) once said: 'The one who is not generous to his guests is not a true follower of Muhammad nor of Ibrāhīm, may Allah bless them both.'[42]

How can such attitude be applied in our day and age? Even in the presence of hotels and restaurants, we should ensure that our communities are as hospitable and welcoming as our dear Prophets Ibrāhīm and Muhammad, may Allah bless them both, were. Moreover, another hadith in Bukhari mentions the rights of visitors '*and your visitors have a right upon you*'.

ACTION ITEMS AND FURTHER DISCUSSION

1. Such manners and good behaviour are best taught by example and through interactions with teachers and mentors. Imam Mālik once said, 'My mother used to dress me before I went to my classes and would say, 'Go to Rabī'ah and learn from his *adab* before his knowledge.'[43]

   We see many hadith describe the manners of Prophet Muhammad, may Allah bless him and give

42 Ibn Rajab, '*Jami' al-'ulum wa-al-hikam*', (Dar Ibn Kathir, 2008).

43 Al-Qadi Iyad, *Tartib al-Madarik wa Taqreeb al-Masalik*, (Dar Al Kutub Al-Ilmiyyah, Beirut, 1997).

him peace, from those who had frequent encounters with him. He walked the walk before talking the talk. And it is enough to cite the praise he got from Allah Almighty:

Most certainly, yours is a sublime character. (al-Qalam 68: 4)

2. Islam's definition of community service, as taught by this Hadith and others, may seem too simplistic for those who may aspire for their impact to reach the whole world. It is great to think beyond oneself and care about the oppressed around the world, but that love and mercy should start with those whom we interact with on a regular basis. In fact, the ideal community that Islam thrives to build is a well-connected one. Those who live inside it do not think of leaving it, after they experience the generosity and honour from their neighbours. Even those who visit such community, the visitors, feel welcome and at home. They may have a variety of social classes and income levels, and they may even have extremely wealthy families living side-by-side with extremely poor ones.

   The ideal community that Islam strives to build is a well-connected one. Those who live inside it do not think of leaving it, as they have seen as having noble character by their neighbours. Those who visit it feel welcome and at home. They may have a variety of social classes and income levels, and they may even have extremely wealthy families living side-by-side with extremely poor ones. However, the latter will never sleep with an empty stomach: *Ibn 'Abbās (RA) reported that the Prophet, may Allah bless him and send him peace, said, 'He is not a believer whose stomach is filled while the neighbour to his side goes hungry.'* (Bayhaqī)

And the closer the neighbour is, the better the relationship must be: *''Ā'ishah, may Allah be pleased with her, once asked the Messenger, may Allah bless him and send him peace, "I have two neighbours, which one should I gift?" And he answered, "To the one with a closer door to yours."'*

3. Activists may tend to prioritize community events, educational circles and service to strangers over family, friends and neighbours. A part of our worship and submission to Allah is to prioritize what Allah Almighty prioritized, even if you aspire towards higher endeavours and more critical roles. Just consider the following *āyah* and how Allah mentions in remarkable detail specific people around us who should receive our *iḥsān:*

   Worship God; join nothing with Him. Be good to your parents, to relatives, to orphans, to the needy, to neighbours near and far, to travellers in need, and to your slaves. God does not like arrogant, boastful people. (al-Nisā' 4: 36)

CHAPTER 6

THE HOW [2]

THE *FIQH* OF ACTIVISM

ACCORDING TO ISLAMIC principles, doing things right is as important as doing the right thing. Muslim activists with the right intention—the *Why*—engage in righteous deeds in social and political spheres—the *What*—should also ensure the practice of submission to Allah, glorified and exalted is He, in *How* they do all that.

The *fiqh* aspect in Islam determines the ruling of certain acts, whether they are required (*fard*), recommended (Sunnah), permissible (*ḥalāl*), disliked (*makrūh*), or unlawful (*ḥarām*).

In Islam, morality is not subject to the whims and the perspectives of people, and true righteousness can only be defined by what pleases Allah, glorified and exalted is He. A Muslim who submits to his Creator accepts the terms and conditions of that contract of *tawḥīd* with Allah, glorified and exalted is He, and ensures that all actions are done in a way that pleases Him:

> **By your Lord, they will not be true believers until they let you decide between them in all matters of dispute, and find no resistance in their souls to your decisions, accepting them totally.** (al-Nisā' 4: 65)

Muslim activists should submit to the authority of the Islamic law, Shariah, firstly by showing submission to the sovereignty of Allah over His creation, and then by following the path of His Messenger Muhammad, may Allah bless him and give him peace. It is not enough to claim to have a Muslim identity if that identity does not involve faith and submission both in theory and in practice. This chapter refers to some hadith that are needed in navigating the complexities of political activism and how a Muslim can ensure commitment in submission to Allah's command as much as possible.

HADITH 29
THE END DOES NOT JUSTIFY THE MEANS

عَنْ أَبِي هُرَيْرَةَ رَضِيَ اللهُ عَنْهُ قَالَ: قَالَ رَسُولُ اللَّهِ صلى الله عليه و سلم 'إِنَّ اللَّهَ طَيِّبٌ لَا يَقْبَلُ إِلَّا طَيِّبًا، وَإِنَّ اللَّهَ أَمَرَ الْمُؤْمِنِينَ بِمَا أَمَرَ بِهِ الْمُرْسَلِينَ فَقَالَ تَعَالَى:

'يَا أَيُّهَا الرُّسُلُ كُلُوا مِنَ الطَّيِّبَاتِ وَاعْمَلُوا صَالِحًا'، وَقَالَ تَعَالَى: 'يَا أَيُّهَا الَّذِينَ آمَنُوا كُلُوا مِنْ طَيِّبَاتِ مَا رَزَقْنَاكُمْ' ثُمَّ ذَكَرَ الرَّجُلَ يُطِيلُ السَّفَرَ أَشْعَثَ أَغْبَرَ يَمُدُّ يَدَيْهِ إِلَى السَّمَاءِ: يَا رَبِّ! يَا رَبِّ! وَمَطْعَمُهُ حَرَامٌ، وَمَشْرَبُهُ حَرَامٌ، وَمَلْبَسُهُ حَرَامٌ، وَغُذِّيَ بِالْحَرَامِ، فَأَنَّى يُسْتَجَابُ لَهُ؟'.

Abū Hurayrah (RA) reported that the Messenger of Allah, peace and blessings be upon him, said: 'O people, Allah is pure and He accepts only what is pure. Verily, Allah has commanded the believers as He commanded His messengers. Allah said, **'O messengers, eat from pure things and act righteously, for I know what you do.'** (al-Mu'minūn 23: 51) *And Allah said,* **'O you who believe, eat from the pure things We have provided for you.'** (al-Baqarah 2: 172) *Then, the Prophet mentioned a man who travelled far, becoming dishevelled and dusty and he raises his hands to the sky, saying, 'O Lord! O Lord!' while his food is unlawful, his drink is unlawful, his clothing is unlawful, and he is nourished by the unlawful, so how can he be answered?* (Muslim)

COMMENTARY

The question of the ends versus the means is brought up in many areas of our complicated modern-day life. Before delving into political activism, one can start with a clear Islamic axiom: that Allah does not repel evil with evil, but only repels evil with what is pure. Prophet Muhammad, may Allah bless him and give him peace, said in part of a long hadith that was narrated by Ibn Mas'ūd, *'Allah does not wipe out evil with evil, but only wipes out evil with that which is pure.'* (Aḥmad)[44]

This basic principle may be used as grounds to navigate other dilemmas, such as:

- Accepting a high position at an unethical company with the intention to use the connections and the networking aspect to reduce the harm produced.
- Joining a political party that has oppressive or immoral stances, while striving to have a seat at the table.
- Hosting a public figure at an event who has disagreeable views about Islamic tenets, including living an immoral lifestyle, openly supporting oppressive regimes, or endorsing major violations of Islamic principles.
- Supporting civil rights groups who may advocate lifestyles that contradict basic tenets of the Muslim faith, such as groups calling to normalize unchaste lifestyles. This may be justified as returning the favour of such groups in supporting Muslim civil rights causes, on the basis of quid pro quo.

All these cases involve some benefit to the Muslim community, but with some level of compromise to our value system. Being in the room with decision-makers is always beneficial but may indicate some level of endorsement and being a witness to injustice (as in hadith 12). A noted public figure with problematic views may attract a bigger audience to events, but may also taint the values and the educational message that the organization stands for. Additionally, working with allies towards a common goal may cause the

44 This narration is rated as weak according to al-Albānī.

Muslim community to accept and normalize un-Islamic lifestyles, and they may eventually become unfaithful to the very essence of their teaching.

The reader is referred to credible scholarly bodies, such as the Assembly of Muslim Jurists of America[45] for a deeper insight on the *fiqh* of necessity (*ḍarūrah*) and the *fiqh* of calamity (*al-nawāzil*). While it may be hard to unite the Muslim voices on the issue of political engagement, the hadith at hand may be used as a starting point to suggest the following:

- Allah only accepts what is pure! This should invite us to take a step backwards and ask ourselves: why did we engage in activism and community work to begin with? If we are sincere in seeking acceptance from Allah, as in hadith 1, then we should put Allah at the centre of our decision-making process, not only for the sake of spiritual motivation.
- In addition to the rewards in the Hereafter, Muslims firmly believe that our efforts will not come to fruition if Allah does not put spiritual goodness (*barakah*) in them. Our fundraising events, political lobbying and educational events would be void of any worldly benefit if Allah does not put His Divine blessings in them. Raising money, organizing a lecture or voting at an election are only a needed first step in the grand scheme of things. As Muslims, we trust that Allah is the Changemaker, and He is the One who will nurture such seeds and bring them to fruition. If we resort to dishonest and unethical means,

45 Assembly of Muslim Jurists of America (AMJA), https://www.amjaonline.org/.

it is unlikely that such work could have any long-lasting effect.

- Acting out of good intentions and performing incomplete acts of worship are not enough! This hadith described a man who is supposedly sincere and humble in his prayer but has made severe violations of Divine law in terms of his income. This resulted in him losing the acceptance and blessings of Allah. This should invite us to include Allah's commands in the *How* as much as the *Why*.
- Muslims submit to the notion that Allah knows what is better for us:

> **How could He who created not know His own creation, when He is the Most Subtle, the All Aware?** (al-Mulk 67: 14)

This shall invite us to firmly believe that the impermissible is inherently bad and harmful, in the short- or the long-term. It may have obvious or hidden consequences, on the individual or on the community or both. Moreover, the impermissible could have some benefit, but the harm will always outweigh the benefit, as in the case of alcohol:

> **They ask you (Prophet) about intoxicants and gambling: say, 'There is great sin in both, and some benefit for people: the sin is greater than the benefit.'** (al-Baqarah 2: 219)

FURTHER DISCUSSION

1. Muslim activists who live in a world that is heavily influenced with notions of modernity should get accustomed to the word *haram* just as they want to hear words of encouragement and support. A huge imbalance of our era is when we refrain from using or hearing any negative comments or critique, and eventually filter out such words from our terminology and our speeches. It is true that some voices within the Muslim community have wrongly and excessively claimed everything to be *haram*, without knowledge. However, we should not react to such bias by going to the other extreme. The prohibitions of Islam should be viewed as safety precautions that our Creator has put for us, Who knows us better than we know ourselves (al-Mulk 67: 14).

2. As much as we invite our community to be open-minded and engage in the political system, elections, and civic engagement, we should also be open-minded about other forms of speaking truth to power. We should realize that voting and civic engagement is a means to an end, and should continuously question the assumptions and the alliances that have been made before.

3. Sometimes the harm associated with certain careers, political engagements or community choices is unavoidable. Credible scholars who are well-

versed in the Islamic Shariah and in the political system will need to identify the harm and assess its intensity. Such an assessment considers the objectives of the Shariah—preservation of people's religion, lives, lineage, intellect, and wealth. It also differentiates between cases of emergency, such as direct and imminent harm on the community, compared to political gains. One should also keep in mind the harm involved with no political action, as it is wrong to assume that such a position is the safest course to preserve one's religion and values (more on this in the discussion on hadith 31).

HADITH 30
DEALING WITH GREY AREAS

عن النعمان بن بشير رضي الله عنهما قال: سمعت رسول الله صلى الله عليه وسلم يقول: 'إن الحلال بين، وإن الحرام بين، وبينهما مشتبهات لا يعلمهن كثير من الناس، فمن اتقى الشبهات، استبرأ لدينه وعرضه، ومن وقع فى الشبهات، وقع فى الحرام، كالراعى يرعى حول الحمى يوشك أن يرتع فيه ألا وإن لكل ملك حمى، ألا وإن حمى الله محارمه، ألا وإن فى الجسد مضغة إذا صلحت صلح الجسد كله، وإذا فسدت فسد الجسد كله: ألا وهى القلب' (متفق عليه)

Al-Nu'mān ibn Bashīr (RA) reported: The Messenger of Allah, peace and blessings be upon him, said: 'What is lawful is clear and what is unlawful is clear, but between them are certain doubtful matters which many people do not know. Thus, he who avoids doubtful matters will preserve his religion and his honour, and he who falls into doubtful matters will fall into the unlawful. This is like the example of a shepherd who pastures his flock close to a sanctuary, all but grazing therein. Indeed, every king has a sanctuary that should be protected. With regards to Allah, His sanctuary is the limits that He has declared unlawful. Truly, the human body holds a piece of flesh that if pure will make the whole body pure, and if corrupt will make the whole body corrupt. This piece of flesh is the human heart.' (Bukhari and Muslim)

COMMENTARY

As the previous hadith (hadith 29) teaches, Muslims may not use an impermissible means even if the outcome and goal is a noble one. However, what about complicated situations when it is unclear whether something is *halal* or *haram*? This is where the hadith at hand becomes very instrumental in teaching one of the basic tenets of the jurisprudence (*fiqh*) of activism on dealing with doubtful matters:

- The default position on all worldly, non-ritual things is permissibility, unless some clear statement in the Qur'an or the Sunnah indicates otherwise, for example, see *al-Baqarah* 2:172-173.
- There will be issues between the halal and the haram that cannot clearly and easily be identified by the layman. The hadith defines them as a a source of confusion and lack of clarity (*shubuhāt*).
- It is not part of the prophetic approach to rush to conclusions and hasten to declare certain issues as haram. Muslims should realize that doing so does not make

someone more righteous or scholarly, as Sufyān al-Thawrī once mentioned, 'True knowledge is manifested by promoting exoneration and ease accompanied with solid proof, as issuing strict and stringent fatwas can be done by anyone.'[46]

- The language here confirms that, while many people may now distinguish doubtful matters, some people will know. The hadith does not indicate that such doubtful matters are completely unknown and mysterious. Muslim scholars are in fact encouraged to investigate and research such matters as long as such effort (*ijtihād*) is done within well-known guidelines and rules. When the Prophet, may Allah bless him and give him peace, sent Muʿādh (RA) to Yemen, he asked him: *On what are you going to base your judgement among the people? Muʿādh said, 'I will judge according to what is in the Book of Allah.' The Prophet said: 'What if it is not in the Book of Allah?' Muʿādh said, 'Then with the tradition (Sunnah) of the Messenger of Allah.' The Prophet said: 'What if it is not in the tradition of the Messenger of Allah?' Muʿādh said, 'Then I will strive to form an opinion* (ijtihād).*' The Prophet said: 'All praise is due to Allah who has made suitable the messenger of the Messenger of Allah.'* (Tirmidhī)
- When the ruling is unclear on a matter, protecting oneself from indulging in the grey areas is always the safer option; consequently, dwelling on doubtful matters may eventually result in becoming immersed in multiple layers of *haram* actions and environments.
- A sound and pure heart that is connected to the revelation is the final arbitrator when the situation involves one

46 Al-Nawawi, *Aadaab Al-Fatwa Wal Mufti Wal Mustafti*, (Dar Al-Fikr, Syria, 1988).

person and his/her choices in life; activists, after they consult with credible scholars, should ensure that they are not indulging in such doubtful matters for the sake of desire, fame, or convenience.

- For communal matters that affect a larger population, such as policy making, it is a bigger challenge to distinguish the *halal* from the *haram*. Other factors come in to play, such as bringing communal benefit (*maṣlaḥah*) and removing harm (*mafsadah*). In these discussions, the context and the assumptions of the political situation and consequences of one's decisions become very critical. Moreover, the discussion shifts into assessing the size of the benefit or harm, and whether it is temporary or permanent. It goes without saying that such benefit should take into account the Muslim *ummah* at large, or at least the Muslim community, not the benefit of the political group or organization or candidate.

ACTION ITEMS

1. Respect the knowledge, experience and wisdom of credible scholars who may have spent a lifetime researching complex topics. Don't assume that a five-minute search on the internet or a couple of lectures are enough to formulate a judgement on such matters. In the meantime, feel free to respectfully ask your teachers and discuss fully the reasoning and the background of their conclusion. Imam Mālik (RA) once said, 'Every person's words may be accepted or rejected, except the man laying

down in that grave,' when referring to the Messenger of Allah, may Allah bless him and give him peace.

2. Using the terminology of this hadith, Muslim activists should differentiate between the clearly *haram* matters from the sources of confusion and lack of clarity (*shubuhāt*). As an example, a Muslim who accepts and normalizes same-sex marriage is in clear violation to Islamic principles. However, working within a specific political party or framework is not as clear, since the context, assumptions and expectations of that alliance are not well-defined.

3. Another important note is to avoid shaming those who differ with us in their *fiqhī* opinion, as long as they did not deviate from the boundaries of mainstream Islamic schools of thought. If we have to engage in a debate, we should keep it professional and maintain our Muslim manners while doing so. Even if we believe the other position is clearly false, this should not result in us maligning their intentions, as 'Alī ibn Abī Ṭālib, may Allah be pleased with him, once said, 'The one who aims for truth but misses it cannot be equated with those who aim for falsehood and get it right.'

4. The Messenger, may Allah bless him and give him peace, advised that one should maintain a clear distance from doubtful matters, even when getting

the most eloquent of answers and opinions to justify the permissibility of something:

'Wābiṣah, *seek consultation with your heart, for righteousness is what the heart and the soul feel easy with, and sin is what throws doubt into the heart, and keeps echoing in the chest. Stick to this method even if people kept issuing rulings (fatwas) at you left and right.'* (narrated by Mundhirī in *al-Targhīb wa'l-Tarhīb*)

Al-Qurṭubī comments on this: Consulting the heart is acceptable from the one whose heart is enlightened with knowledge, and whose limbs were adorned with abstinence from the unlawful. This is because only such people have the ability to sense the traces of the doubtful matter in their hearts to begin with. Otherwise, the following statement from Sulaymān al-Taymī, may Allah have mercy on him, is profoundly cautionary, 'If you were to take permissions and exceptions from each scholar (or may we say, the mistake of each scholar) then you have allowed all the evils to accumulate in your heart.'[47]

---

47 Abou Nou'aym Al-Asfahani, *Hilyat al-awliya wa tabaqat al-asfiya*, (Dar Al Kutub Al-Ilmiyyah, Beirut, 1988).

HADITH 31
WORKING WITHIN CAPACITY

عَنْ عَائِشَةَ، عَنِ النَّبِيِّ صلى الله عليه وسلم قَالَ ' سَدِّدُوا وَقَارِبُوا، وَأَبْشِرُوا، فَإِنَّهُ لاَ يُدْخِلُ أَحَدًا الْجَنَّةَ عَمَلُهُ '. قَالُوا وَلاَ، أَنْتَ يَا رَسُولَ اللَّهِ قَالَ ' وَلاَ أَنَا إِلاَّ أَنْ يَتَغَمَّدَنِي اللَّهُ بِمَغْفِرَةٍ وَرَحْمَةٍ '.

'Ā'ishah narrates that the Prophet, may Allah bless him and give him peace, said: 'Aspire for the best deeds, maintain a sense of moderation, and stay positive and hopeful in your Lord, for your deeds alone are not enough to earn you Paradise.' When the Companions heard that, they said, 'Not even you, O Messenger of Allah'? He said, 'Not even I, but only when Allah envelops me with His mercy.' (Bukhārī)

COMMENTARY

The Muslim values needed for activism and community work, such as *iḥsān,* analyzed in hadith 26, as well as integrity in hadith 29, are often confronted by the realities of our world: multiple layers of oppression and injustice, a considerable loss of moral direction in humanity at large and a huge amount of confusion and misinformation. This has resulted in very limited avenues that can be sought to effect real change. Consequently, genuine and caring people may start doubting themselves.

- Why should I bother teaching my students and improve their behaviour, if their parents do not want them to change and if the society around them is shaping their behaviour more than lectures and classes do?

- What good would my charity do in the face of all the poverty, turmoil and wars that this country is facing?
- How far can my political engagement go if the whole system is corrupt? Is there even any place for principled activism in the chaotic and opportunistic jungle of politics?
- How can one enjoin good and forbid evil in the case of voting for a favourable candidate who may have some disagreeable policies and stances? What is the Islamic guidance on aiming for partial or uncertain goals in the process?

While a complete answer is beyond the scope of this book, this hadith can provide some guidance on the following:

- A Muslim is responsible for the effort, not the outcome. Muslim activists should exert their ultimate capacity:
  God does not burden any soul with more than it can bear. (al-Baqarah 2: 286)
- Our deeds, whether they are related to ritualistic acts of worship, community service, or activism, should aim at the ultimate and the most sought-after outcome, which is entering Paradise. Such deeds are, in themselves, not enough to enter Paradise, and it is only due to Allah's mercy that one can earn His forgiveness. This alone should stop us from putting our faith in our deeds and actions, and relieve us from the distress of sometimes *not* seeing our work achieve the outcomes we sought.

Instead of looking at results, the hadith commands us to focus on:

- *Saddidū:* doing the right thing, have the right mindset and opinion, to plan while doing the good deed. The Arabic word is normally used when aiming an arrow towards a specific target and hitting it. So, when it comes to our intention and our vision of what needs to be done, there is no room for an incomplete, deviant or morally wrong attempt to do good (as hadith 29 teaches).

- *Qāribū*: from the Arabic word for *near* (*qarīb*) as in having one's arrow being sent as near as possible to its target. Normally for an arrow to stay on its trajectory, it has to be handled with a balanced approach: the bow has to be held firmly but without excessive tension on the string; the arrow speed and force should take into account the wind speed, weight of the arrow, proximity of the target, etc. The language here, according to Ibn Rajab, suggests that we should be moderate in our acts of worship, without the two extremes of being too intense or too complacent.

Between *saddidū* and *qāribū*, Ibn Rajab has a profound statement that beautifully captures the prophetic wisdom and balanced approach:

Qāribū refers to the result of your arrow reaching the vicinity of the bullseye, even if the target itself was not hit. On the other hand, *saddidū* reflects that you started with a pure intention that does not settle for less. You have aimed for the right goal, and that is what matters even if you unintentionally missed the target.

Back to the question at hand, advocating for the lesser of two evils in politics and removing whatever harm or damage within your capacity does not necessarily equate to selling out on Islamic principles. As long as we realize that such a situation is an exception, and we always keep a mindset of *saddidū*, of continuously pushing the boundaries and raising the bar, we are allowed in Islam to work within a *qāribū* framework.

It is worth noting that a similar rule exists in other areas of Islamic jurisprudence (*fiqh*), such as the prayer of a disabled person, as in the hadith: '*Pray while standing, and if you are not able, then while seated, and if you cannot, then lay down.*' (Bukhari)

The inability to fulfil all the elements of the prayer (standing up) is not an excuse for a sick person not to perform what is within their capacity. Our scholars derived multiple maxims of *fiqh* that are important in guiding these discussions:

- What can be done with ease is not dropped because of what only can be done with hardship.
- What cannot be attained in its entirety cannot be abandoned as a whole.
- Difficulty in implementation brings out a relief in ruling.

ACTION ITEMS AND FURTHER DISCUSSION

1. The prophetic mindset of *qāribū* should guide us to stay away from the black and white, all-or-nothing mentality when untangling complicated issues in activism and community work. Allah says in the Qur'an: **So fear Allah as much as you are able and listen and obey and spend (in the way of Allah); it is better for your selves.** (al-Taghābun 64: 16)

How does this translate into our activism? One cannot advise a Muslim woman about proper Islamic dress code by using the argument, 'You either wear the 100% modest dress code, or you better not wear the hijab at all.' Or to tell a brother, 'You either correct all of your manners and behaviour or you should not get involved in community service.'

2. Never use this hadith as a justification for being mediocre. *Iḥsān* and excellence cannot be stressed enough (hadith 26):

   Who listen to what is said and follow what is best. These are the ones God has guided; these are the people of understanding. (al-Zumar 39: 18)

3. One cannot fully understand and apply the hadith to activism while sitting on the side-lines and postulating theories of what and how things should be done. The whole framework of the 40 hadith on activism encourages us to do the work, become involved in matters, engage in discussions, and seek prophetic wisdom before, during and after doing the work. Our rich Islamic tradition should push us towards finding real solutions, and not engage only in intellectual battles and theories, or to mistakenly use Islam as a hindrance towards doing good.

4. When assessing harm versus benefit of an issue, our scholars stress the point that removing the

harm takes a priority over bringing benefits. This should enable us to cautiously handle rulings on exceptions and not overstretch them and make them an umbrella to legitimize Islamic violations. Abū Hurayrah (RA) narrated:

I heard the Messenger of Allah, may Allah bless him and give him peace, say, 'What I have forbidden for you, avoid. What I have ordered you (to do), do as much of it as you can. For verily, it was only the excessive questioning and their disagreeing with their Prophets that destroyed (the nations) who were before you.' (Bukhārī and Muslim)

HADITH 32
BUILDING ALLIANCES FOR SOCIAL JUSTICE

عَنْ عَبْدِ الرَّحْمَنِ بْنِ عَوْفٍ ، قَالَ : قَالَ رَسُولُ اللهِ صلى الله عليه وسلم :' شَهِدْتُ حِلْفَ بَنِي هَاشِمٍ ، وَزَهْرَةَ ، وَتَيْمٍ ، فَمَا يَسُرُّنِي أَنِّي نَقَضْتُهُ وَلِيَ حُمْرُ النَّعَمِ ، وَلَوْ دُعِيتُ بِهِ الْيَوْمَ لأَجَبْتُ عَلَى أَنْ نَأْمُرَ بِالْمَعْرُوفِ ، وَنَنْهَى عَنِ الْمُنْكَرِ وَنَأْخُذَ لِلْمَظْلُومِ مِنَ الظَّالِمِ. (البزار في المسند)

In my early years, I witnessed a treaty between the tribes of Banū Hāshim, Banū Zahrah and Banū Taym, and I would never let go of that agreement even if given the finest of camels, and if I were to be invited to such an agreement even after becoming a prophet, I would respond without hesitation, for the sake of enjoining good, forbidding evil, and supporting the oppressed against their oppressors. (Narrated by Bazzār in his *Musnad*)

COMMENTARY

This hadith emphasizes an incident from the Prophet's early life before prophethood that was implanted in his memory for decades: The Treaty of *al-Fuḍūl* (also known as the Treaty of al-*Mutayyibīn*), which was a coalition of different tribes who rarely agreed on anything in public affairs. Still, they joined together to protect the rights of the immigrants and foreigners in Makkah who did not enjoy the political benefits that the ruling tribes enjoyed. Although the hadith talks about an incident before prophethood, it shows the Prophet's willingness to accept such a coalition as a messenger, which gives this hadith a legislative Divine endorsement. This hadith serves as a basis for Muslim activists in political and social spheres to work with other groups and coalitions that aim to support the weak and the oppressed. Having theological or moral disagreements shall not stop us from working on causes that are of mutual interest, and it should not even matter to us who is leading that effort or inviting towards such a coalition. In matters of justice, Allah Almighty encourages the believers to stand firmly against tribalism and ethnocentrism and to always incline towards the truth:

> **You who believe, be steadfast in your devotion to God and bear witness impartially: do not let hatred of others lead you away from justice, but adhere to justice, for that is closer to awareness of God. Be mindful of God: God is well aware of all that you do.** (al-Mā'idah 5: 8)

This hadith shall be understood in the context of other Islamic rules, such as the *ayah*:

> **Help one another towards birr (righteousness) and taqwā (piety), and do not help one another towards sin (ithm) and hostility (ʿudwān).** (al-Māʾidah 5: 2)

Al-Saʿdī gives a detailed analysis of this ayah:

- *Al-birr* here includes all deeds, hidden and public, that Allah loves, in addition to the rights of Allah and the rights of other people.
- The word *taqwā* in this context includes refraining from everything that Allah and His Messenger, may Allah bless him and give him peace, hate.
- *Ithm* refers to overstepping the limits of Allah by doing acts of disobedience.
- *ʿUdwān* is transgressing against people with regards to their lives, wealth, and reputations.

This is why as believers who submit to Allah, we need to ensure that we don't use this hadith as an invitation for unconditional political pragmatism. Instead, we need to consider the following:

WHAT THE TREATY OF AL-FUḌŪL DOES NOT TEACH

- The *al-Fuḍūl* declaration was concerned with basic human rights that everybody agrees on, even those who disagreed on everything else, such as religion, values, and politics. This cannot be extrapolated to become an umbrella to promote all issues that are considered fringe ones to the communities of faith.
- In the context of *al-Fuḍūl*, all the parties involved were transparent and honest in voicing their disagreement on the issues that lay beyond the treaty. The Muslim community should consistently recognize its responsibility to enjoin good and forbid evil by hand, tongue, or at least in their hearts (for more detail, please see the discussion in hadith 12). Without this important element in a community's life, entering into a coalition on generalized terms without clear boundaries may lead to normalizing other people's values or their sins.
- *Al-Fuḍūl* was recognized by the Messenger, may Allah bless him and give him peace, in a position of power (some narrations mention that it happened after the conquest of Makkah). The Muslim community may seek an alliance during a time of weakness; however, this would be a situation of necessity, and shall be understood as an exception instead of being the norm.
- *Al-Fuḍūl* was not invoked to normalize the practices of *Jāhiliyyah*, but to praise specific incidents that Muslims already call for. An educated activist should always be aware of superficial slogans that plague the social justice institutions and the public space. Such slogans mix the

good with the bad, and use agreeable human rights, for example women's rights, as a cover for destructive social change, such as extreme notions of feminism that destroy family unity.

- *Al-Fuḍūl* is a coalition, not a political front or party. By definition, it is temporary in nature, and can be based on a narrow set of agreeable issues while allowing its members to disagree on others.[48]

ACTION ITEMS

1. A famous story in the Arabic literature mentions three bulls who had different skin colours–white, black, and red–but were united against the lion who was their common enemy. Later the lion was able to spread division between them and managed to devour them one by one, starting with the white bull. The last bull standing realized his mistake of not supporting his brethren, but only after it was already too late to do so, and expressed his regret by saying, 'I was attacked on the same day the white bull was attacked!'

2. Read Malcolm X's essay on Palestine as a team, and reflect on his understanding of the intertwined reality of the fight towards social justice for black people as well as the Palestinian people. The agendas of racism, capitalism and colonization are well-connected, and activists who are working

48 Walid, D, *Towards Sacred Activism* (Mecca Books, 2018).

to address some of these issues should understand this reality and maintain some level of cooperation.

3. Ensure that your organization accurately reflects all segments of your community with qualified leaders and representatives, according to ethnic background, social classes, education, as some examples. Creating an environment of inclusion starts with breaking the segregated lines and building bonds with each other. This should push your members to think beyond the issues that pertain to their cultural background, such as racial inequality, refugees from their country or the occupation of Palestine, and care for other causes as well. Other methods include taking a course in the subject, reading history, or preparing a presentation about the cause. The hope is for our community to be knowledgeable, empathetic, and supportive to as many causes as possible and ensure that we are doing so due to our faith, and not political or national identity.

HADITH 33
HANDLING INTERNAL POLITICS AND DIFFERENCES OF OPINION

عَنِ ابْنِ عُمَرَ، قَالَ قَالَ النَّبِيُّ صلى الله عليه وسلم لَنَا لَمَّا رَجَعَ مِنَ الأَحْزَابِ ’ لاَ يُصَلِّيَنَّ أَحَدٌ الْعَصْرَ إِلاَّ فِي بَنِي قُرَيْظَةَ ‘. فَأَدْرَكَ بَعْضُهُمُ الْعَصْرَ فِي الطَّرِيقِ فَقَالَ بَعْضُهُمْ لاَ نُصَلِّي حَتَّى نَأْتِيَهَا، وَقَالَ بَعْضُهُمْ بَلْ

نُصَلِّي لَمْ يُرِدْ مِنَّا ذَلِكَ. فَذُكِرَ لِلنَّبِيِّ صلى الله عليه وسلم فَلَمْ يُعَنِّفْ وَاحِدًا مِنْهُمْ.

Ibn 'Umar (RA) narrates that when the Prophet, may Allah bless him and give him peace, returned from the Battle of al-Aḥzāb, he said to us, 'None should perform the 'Aṣr prayer before we arrive at the land of the Tribe of Qurayẓah.' The sun came close to sunset and the time for prayer was about to end, so some of them decided not to pray until they arrived, whereas others preferred to pray while on the road, claiming that, 'We were literally commanded not to delay the prayer.' The decisions of both sides were mentioned to the Messenger, may Allah bless him and give him peace, who did not rebuke either of them. (Bukhārī)

COMMENTARY

This hadith provides important guidance for Muslim organizations who wish to minimize conflicts and disarray that may result from disagreements in religious opinions, schools of thought, or political views. It is easy for Muslims to trivialize internal politics and differences in the face of external threats and challenges. However, while the latter unite and strengthen the team, the former may destroy physical and spiritual momentum and drain time, energy, and resources. Allah, Glorified and Exalted is He, warns us about the consequences of disarray and conflict:

And obey Allah and His Messenger, and do not dispute and (thus) lose courage and [then] your

> **strength would depart; and be patient. Indeed, Allah is with the patient.** (al-Anfāl 8: 46)

History shows us how clashes between multiple sects can be initiated, especially between those who are more learned in religion. The Qur'an clearly warns against using sacred knowledge as fuel for division and disunity:

> **They divided, out of rivalry, only after knowledge had come to them.** (al-Shūrā 42: 13)

The hadith at hand refers to an incident after the Battle of the Confederates (*al-Aḥzāb*) when the Messenger of Allah, may Allah bless him and give him peace, encouraged the Companions to march immediately to the fortress of the Tribe of Qurayẓah. Events on the ground dictated that the Muslim army move quickly, without taking a break in Madinah even for the the mid-afternoon prayer (*ṣalāt al-'aṣr*). However, it was unclear whether the command was meant to be taken literally, as it is forbidden to pray before everyone arrives at their destination, or metaphorically, to respect the need to move quickly. The Companions themselves, may Allah be pleased with all of them, understood the prophetic command differently, and this apparently caused some confusion. Some were concerned about missing the prayer and performed it on the road, while others chose to stick literally to the command and prayed upon their arrival, which happened after the time of the evening prayer (*ṣalāt al-'ishā'*) had started. What is remarkable is the maturity and unity the Companions showed during the whole process. We did not see one party accusing the other of defying the

Sunnah or being negligent with the prayer time! The cause and the mission that united them all was more critical than such differences, and they realized that their disagreements should not distract them from their main goal.

The purpose of this discussion is to highlight that we should not trivialize our disagreements, nor establish superficial harmony under the slogans of brotherhood and unity. A genuinely functional team ensures that all voices are heard and all positions are well-represented.[49] We should critique all credible ideas and arguments without pushing anybody to feel defensive and eventually take things to a personal level. As Imam al-Nasāfī (RA) once said:

> In minor issues of the faith, if we are asked about our position as compared to those who disagree with us, we say that our opinion is right but could be wrong, while the opposing position is wrong but could be right. Otherwise, we would not acknowledge that a person of *ijtihad* may reach right or wrong conclusions. On the other hand, in case we are asked about our creed and our faith, we ought to say that we are upon the truth, and our opponents are on nothing but falsehood.[50]

---

49 Lencioni, P., and Okabayashi, K., *The five dysfunctions of a team: An illustrated leadership fable*, Hoboken, (N.J: Wiley, 2008).

50 Ibn Nujaym, *Ashbah wa'l-Nazai'r ala Madhhab Abi Hanifah Al-Nu'man,* (Dar Al Kutub Al-Ilmeyyah, 1999). This quote is also famously attributed to Imam Shāfiʿī.

FURTHER DISCUSSIONS

1. The discussion on tolerance of other opinions shall not lead the Muslim community to adopt or normalise fringe opinions and positions. Community activists and leaders should be aware of the framework and boundaries that the scholars of the *ummah* have established for centuries. We should not fall into oversimplification of deep scholarly issues that experienced scholars have researched for decades, and bypass all of that with opinions that are based on superficial readings of a few articles online. As an actionable item, consider having an advisory board of credible scholars who can help the team navigate through complex discussions.

2. Muslim activists and organizations should reflect deeply on the divided nature of the Muslim *ummah* on the larger scale (of countries and governments) or even on the smaller scale (local organizations and institutes). In addition to the natural tendency of human beings to become divided and separated, the Muslim *ummah* should realize that Divine intervention in this regard is not guaranteed. The Prophet Muhammad, may Allah bless him and give him peace, pleaded to Allah to protect us from trials and tribulations that stem from our differences. However, this specific prayer was not granted. In an authentic hadith in *Ṣaḥīḥ Muslim*, the Prophet asked Allah to protect the Muslim *ummah* from

three forms of trial and tribulation. However, and for a wisdom that only Allah Glorified and Exalted knows, He chose to leave it up to human beings to navigate such differences:

'Āmir ibn Sa'd (RA) reported on the authority of his father that one day the Messenger of Allah, may Allah bless him and give him peace, travelled from the neighbouring heights of Madinah and stopped by the mosque of the Tribe of Mu'awiyah to pray two rak'ahs, *and we all followed him in prayer. He then started making a long supplication to His Master, and, after he finished, he came to us and said, 'I asked Allah for three requests. He granted me two of them but He withheld one. I asked Him to protect my* ummah *from being destroyed completely due to famine, and He granted me this. Then I asked Allah to protect my* ummah *from completely being drowned in a flood, and He granted me this. Then I asked Allah to protect my ummah from directing their conflicts and fights towards each other, but He did not grant me this request.'* (Muslim)

3. The discussion on tolerance and acceptance of opposing viewpoints should not lead us to shy away from difficult conversations to be had when addressing these issues. We should always strive for a balanced approach where we: (i) cooperate in the areas of agreement; (ii) excuse each other on the 'tolerable' areas of disagreement; and (iii) voice our disagreements boldly but respectfully when it comes to what we perceive as violations. As an example, let

us consider an instructive disagreement between two noble Prophets, Aaron and Moses, peace be upon them:

[Aaron] said, 'O son of my mother, indeed the people oppressed me and were about to kill me, so let not the enemies rejoice over me and do not place me among the wrongdoing people.' (al-Aʿrāf 7: 150)

This incident occurred while Moses was absent from his community for forty days, during which the community began to worship the calf. Aaron went out of his way to save the faith of his people and invite them back to Allah. However, they tried to kill him, so he chose to remain silent and keep the community together so they wouldn't wander around in the desert. Contrary to what some people think, Aaron did not approve of their worship to prioritize their unity over their faith. Without this understanding, we may end up assuming that the ultimate goal of activism is the unity of the Muslim community, while we forget that it is essential to understand what we are uniting upon. Ibn Ḥajar (RA) puts this beautifully in this statement:

When matters of disagreement arise, we shall not shy away from addressing them by staying in our homes and breaking our swords. By doing so, no command of Allah would ever be followed, no evil would ever be stopped and the people of sin would find an easy way to commit their evil. From violating people's properties and lives to promoting various forms of injustice, Muslims shall not say that such a situation is a matter of trial and tribulation (*fitnah*)—we were commanded to avoid indulging in it. Clearly, this contradicts essential teachings of Islam in stopping the wrongdoers and the foolish from spreading harm on the earth.[51]

51 Ibn Hajar, *Fath al-Bari bi Sharh Sahih al-Bukhari*, (Dar Al-Risalah Al-Alamiyah , Beirut 2013).

CHAPTER 7

THE WHILE

GUIDE FOR SELF-CARE AND PROTECTION FROM BURNOUT

IT IS VERY easy for Muslims who are striving to initiate social and political change to feel overwhelmed and exhausted from the endless challenges facing the Muslim community. On a global level, we are bombarded with pictures of war, destruction, turmoil, and political unrest, in addition to poverty, natural disasters, and the list goes on. At a local level, those who step up for leadership immediately become magnets for anyone asking for donation, seeking advice, or just complaining about community issues. For this reason, activists and community organizers need to be reminded on a consistent basis that the goals they work for are in the hands of Allah.

According to a Muslim's belief system, change can only come from Allah, He is the only changemaker, not other people, be they individuals or organizations. Our actions, however, are part of our worldly test that may invite such change as in the *ayah*:

> **Indeed, Allah will not change the condition of a people until they change what is in themselves.** (al-Raʿd 13: 11)

Al-Saʿdī comments on this by saying:

> Allah does not change a people's condition of prosperity had they not shifted from faith to disbelief, from obedience to sin, or from gratitude for Allah's blessings to insolence because of them. In such ways, Allah takes those blessings away from them. By the same token, if people change their condition of sin, and shift towards obedience to Allah, Allah will change the miserable situation in which they were to one of blessing, happiness, joy, and mercy.

The 40 hadith on community service and activism collection concludes with the hadith on self-care with essential messages to every activist and leader: stay positive and hopeful, do not ignore your personal growth and emotional well-being, and keep on planting your seeds of change in a consistent and hopeful manner. At the end of the day, your service to the community is nothing but a means of self-purification, and your battle against injustice should start with your own whims, desires and negative thoughts.

HADITH 34
INVEST IN YOURSELF

عن أبي هريرة رضي الله عنه قال: قال رسول الله صلى الله عليه وسلم: 'المؤمن القوي خير وأحب إلى الله من المؤمن الضعيف وفي كل خير. احرص على ما ينفعك، واستعن بالله ولا تعجز. وإن أصابك شيء فلا تقل: لو أني فعلت كان كذا وكذا، ولكن قل: قدر الله، وما شاء فعل؛ فإن لو تفتح عمل الشيطان' (رواه مسلم)

Abū Hurayrah reported that the Messenger of Allah, peace and blessings be upon him, said: The strong believer is better and more beloved to Allah than the weak believer, and both of them have goodness. Be eager for what benefits you, seek help from Allah, and do not be frustrated or lazy. If something befalls you, then do not say if only I had done something else. Rather say that Allah has decreed what He wills. Verily, the phrase 'if only' opens the way for the work of Satan. (Muslim)

COMMENTARY

Muslims who volunteer their free time for the community should not be distracted from their personal journey of self-development in all aspects of life. After all, the best way to help the Muslim community is to empower more strong Muslims, starting with your own self. The wording in the early part of the hadith is generic and may be applied to different dimensions of strength: Seeking physical strength, financial independence, intellectual competence, and spiritual resilience are all desirable traits that Prophet

Muhammad, may Allah bless him and give him peace, wanted for his community. However, the hadith later focuses on spiritual strength as the most important outcome of other worldly dimensions of strength. Imam Nawawī, may Allah have mercy on him, elaborates on this:

> Strength here refers to the determination of the soul while pushing it to the affairs of the Hereafter. The one with such a trait unleashes with bravery against the enemies in the battlefield, speeds up while approaching them and even seeks these enemies out. Through courage and strength, this person becomes motivated to enjoin good and forbid evil, while patiently bearing all hardship in the path of Allah. Finally, this person feels noble desire for acts of worship, such as praying, fasting, and remembrance, and is consistent in doing so.

From this perspective, we can understand how strong believers seek spiritual strength in their worldly matters:

- Strong believers, in the physical sense, have the courage and the ability to defend themselves and others against any oppression (as in hadith 13). They have more energy and stamina to worship Allah without any laziness, as explained beautifully by Imam Nawawī further on in his commentary: *'ʿĀ'ishah, may Allah be pleased with her, narrated that the Messenger of Allah, may Allah bless him and give him peace, used to take a nap until he heard the first* adhān, *then he would spring up for the prayer.'* (Muslim)
- Strong believers in the financial sense give more in charity, are more likely to take calculated risks in business, and

eventually form strong and independent communities that are not subservient to others (as hadith 39 teaches).

- Believers who are strong intellectually and academically are firm in their faith against misconceptions and doubts that others can throw against one's faith. They approach every commitment with *iḥsān* (as in hadith 26) and use their position and their career to support their families and society at large.
- Strong believers, on the social side, are well-connected to the community and establish a meaningful relationship with their friends and family. They have a strong sense of belonging and identity and give back as much as they receive from others. This support system (as described in hadith 27) protects against potential harms that may come from dealing with others (as in hadith 21).

ACTION ITEMS

1. This hadith presents a blueprint for attaining strength in all its forms. It gives practical advice on what a strong believer should pursue before, during, and after a certain activity:

    a. *Be eager for what benefits you*: Begin with the very end in mind (as in hadith 1) and set the right intention and mindset.

    b. *Seek help from Allah*: Make *du'ā'* consistently in all of your matters—whether it is for personal goals, community service or career aspirations.

Realize that your own strength or willpower will not get you anywhere without Allah's help (as in hadith 5).

c. *Don't be lazy or give up*: There is no substitute for hard work. Work hard and without leaving any stone unturned. This is the physical and material dimension that should accompany any spiritual preparatory work.

d. *In case something happens to you*: Instead of blaming yourself and lamenting previous decisions, realize that success as you define it is not guaranteed, and that Allah has a better plan for you. As long as you have put in the right amount of effort and have maintained a spiritual connection to Allah, then accept whatever results come from Allah, and submit to His will and decree. That is not to say that one cannot learn from their past decisions and examine whether they could have done any better. However, one shall not let that examination result in a downward spiral of *what if* thoughts and regrets. Instead, realize that Allah decrees outcomes, and whatever He plans and Wills surpasses your human plans and will.

2. The hadith emphasized that there is good in all people of faith, even if they are weak in that faith, and that Allah loves them so long as they have faith in their hearts. It shows how honourable a believer

is in the eyes of Allah, and how much of a difference there is between *īmān* and *kufr*. It motivates and inspires the weak believers to realize that they have some value, and also reminds the strong believer to never look down on or completely disregard a weaker believer for there is good in them too. The following verse shows how different believers will have different capacities and forms of strength, and how Allah allows for each one of them the chance to improve, get better, and serve:

We gave the Scripture as a heritage to Our chosen servants: some of them wronged their own souls, some stayed between [right and wrong], and some, by God's leave, were foremost in good deeds. That is the greatest favour. (Fāṭir 35: 32)

3. The *istikhārah* prayer, the prayer seeking God's guidance, is a very practical implementation of this hadith. It involves (i) goal setting, (ii) prioritizing the Hereafter before the worldly life, (iii) seeking help from Allah, and (iv) being satisfied with whatever Allah chooses for us.

HADITH 35
SPREAD POSITIVITY WITH REALISM

عَنْ أَبِي هُرَيْرَةَ، أَنَّ رَسُولَ اللَّهِ صلى الله عليه وسلم قَالَ ' إِذَا سَمِعْتَ الرَّجُلَ يَقُولُ هَلَكَ النَّاسُ . فَهُوَ أَهْلَكُهُمْ ' . (مسلم)

Mālik related to me from Suhayl ibn Abī Ṣāliḥ from his father from Abū Hurayrah that the Messenger of Allah, may Allah bless him and grant him peace, said: 'When you hear a man say, "The people are ruined," he is the most ruined of them all.' (Muslim)

COMMENTARY

Human beings tend to overly criticize things around them by disproportionately focusing on the negative. This is a commonly observed behaviour between parents and their children, and between spouses who tend to highlight mistakes while ignoring each other's virtues. Criticism, when joined with love and care, is a necesary virtue in the Muslim ethical system (as in hadith 24). However, it is worrisome when the noble act of *naṣīḥah* is transformed into an extreme form of fault-finding.

In community work, those who get deeply involved in an organization and are exposed to its behind-the-scenes workings may become exhausted with the negativity and pessimism they find. This may be manifested as excessive highlighting of the mistakes of leaders and organizations, making destructive criticism of the speeches and lectures of scholars, and eventually being cynical and doubtful about any sincere effort. Such people may start spreading their hopelessness in the community, and, even if they continue to occupy positions inside organizations, they would do so without empathy, love, care or hope for results.

Such tendencies become worrisome when those people give a religious label to their insecurities and doubts. They may start speaking on behalf of Islam, and this causes the general public to buy into these accusations and feel more distant and less confident about their faith.

It is worth noting that the last word of this hadith has been narrated in two different ways, resulting in different but complementary interpretations:

1. *Huwa ahlakuhum*: 'He is the most ruined among them.' According to this narration, the Prophet, may Allah bless him and give him peace, is warning us from passing judgement on people and claiming someone's final destination will be eternal ruination. Clearly, one can point out that someone is misguided due to a specific sin or immoral action, with the intention of giving advice to help that person to change (as in hadith 12 and 24). However, one cannot go beyond that to assume that this person is beyond hope, or that they will never be guided or forgiven by Allah, as in the following hadith:

   Jundub reported that the Messenger of Allah, peace and blessings be upon him, said, "A man said, 'By Allah, Allah will not forgive this person!'" Allah Almighty said, 'Who is he who swore by Me

> *that I will not forgive someone? I have forgiven him and nullified your good deeds.'* (Muslim)

In addition, the person with such an attitude could have evil intent on the inside. His harsh criticisms and spreading of rumours about others may be a projection of his own insecurity and evil deeds on others. As al-Mutanabbī, the famous poet, said:

> *When a man's deeds become evil,*
> *his assumptions will follow through,*
> *And he starts believing what he initially assumed*
> *And he will start taking enemies from his friends,*
> *And in darkness and doubtfulness eventually will be consumed*

2. *Huwa ahlakahum*: 'He has caused them to be ruined.' According to this narration, declaring the whole community to be misguided will create some form of a self-fulfilling prophecy. It may spread hopelessness, pessimism, gloominess, and mistrust among the people, and eventually result in people losing hope in their attempt to repent and improve themselves.

Imam al-Khaṭṭābī has an interesting commentary that can be applied to both meanings: one may keep on highlighting other people's mistakes and listing their shortcomings, by saying that people are corrupt and are ruined, until he is deemed to be the most ruined of them all, because he is worse than all of them due to being sinful in spreading slander and mischief amongst them. This may also cause him to feel arrogant around them, by assuming that he is better than them.

ACTION ITEMS

1. As a leader, one should be careful and cognizant of the amount of positive or negative words and comments they use. In our meetings, public lectures and even in our private thoughts, we should resist that bias to portray things as gloomy and hopeless. On the other hand, this should not result in us propagating false images of perfection. How can one maintain the balance? By making sure that our perspectives and critiques, the positive and the negative, invite more action, collaboration, and motivation. Confront the negatives while rejoicing in all the positives, which are usually more numerous.

2. Teachers and public speakers should maintain a balance in their educational messages, between listing problems and challenges of a community while also providing them with solutions, hope and actionable items. Everyone can pinpoint problems and mistakes, but the true reformers are those who provide solutions and roadmaps for people to get out of these problems.

3. A community member should shut the voice of destructive criticism inside his or her head and count positive things in an event he or she has attended, before moving to the countless observations about the parking lot, the attendance, the microphone, as 'He who does not thank people does not thank Allah.'

4. Reflect on the incident from the *Sīrah* when the Prophet Muhammad, may our souls be sacrificed for his honour, was insulted, attacked and exiled outside of Taif. Despite being in a very critical and weak position in his life, he maintained his attitude of mercy and forgiveness for the very same people who had harmed him, and said in a supplication that was full of hope: *'Maybe Allah will bring out of their offspring those who worship Allah alone.'* (Muslim)

HADITH 36
BE PROACTIVE & PLANT YOUR SEEDS

عَنْ أَنَسِ بْنِ مَالِكٍ، عَنِ النَّبِيِّ صلى الله عليه وسلم قَالَ: إِنْ قَامَتِ السَّاعَةُ وَفِي يَدِ أَحَدِكُمْ فَسِيلَةٌ، فَإِنِ اسْتَطَاعَ أَنْ لاَ تَقُومَ حَتَّى يَغْرِسَهَا فَلْيَغْرِسْهَا. (البخاري)

Anas ibn Malik reported that the Prophet, may Allah bless him and grant him peace, said: 'If the Final Hour comes while you have a sapling palm in your hands and it is possible to plant it before the Hour arrives, you should plant it.' (Bukhārī)

COMMENTARY

This hadith fuses the spiritual and the materialistic aspects of Islam by providing guidance on our priorities should we witness the Day of Judgement unfolding in front of our eyes. Even if we do not live to witness the event, we are taught a very important mindset on how to respond to crises or turmoil of such immensity that we feel helpless and hopeless, such as witnessing a devastating war or living under extreme oppression or discrimination. No tribulation can be more severe than the Day of Judgement itself, that is why this hadith should influence our productivity, goalsetting and plans in any other crisis.

Normally, when a believer reflects on death, the Hereafter and preparing for it, our thought process normally leaps to spiritual or ritual means of preparation, such as prayer, supplication, and donation. While these are noble and righteous deeds, in this hadith the Prophet Muhammad, may Allah bless him and give him peace, is emphasizing that planting a seed and finishing what could be deemed as a 'worldly' act of service is also a priority. This remains true even after you realize that the Day of Judgement is about to start, even if you believed in that moment that nobody would eat from that tree or ever be shaded by it. Even if you believed there would be no oxygen or sunlight left for that tree to grow! The message here is: do your part, and finish planting your seed! You are held accountable for the act itself and how much *iḥsān* you put into it (hadith 26), while its fruits are in the hands of the Almighty.

The more we reflect on farmers and the act of planting seeds, the more we understand how important such a mindset is for those who step up for the difficult task of reforming a community. Planting seeds involve setting goals that are long-term, with no instant gratification or fast and easy wins. It involves consistency in sticking to a process—from watering the plant, nurturing it, to removing threats—more than being fixated on the final product.[52] And finally, it requires a firm belief in the Unseen, in the form of rain, and complete reliance on Allah, who is in full control of the final result:

> **Consider the seeds you sow in the ground, is it you who make them grow or We? If We wished, We could turn your harvest into chaff and leave you to wail, 'We are burdened with debt; rather we are totally deprived.'** (al-Wāqiʿah 56: 63-67)

Building on the previous points, Islam teaches us to be proactive in our deeds and take initiative before trials and tribulations fall upon us, as in the following hadith:

> *Abū Hurayrah (RA) reported that the Messenger of Allah, may Allah bless him and grant him peace, said: 'Hasten to perform good deeds before a tribulation which will be like the dark part of the night, in which a man will be a believer in the morning and an unbeliever in the evening, or he will be a believer in the evening and an unbeliever in the morning. He would sell his faith for some goods in the world.'* (Muslim)

The word *badara* shares the same root word with *badr* which refers to the full moon in the Arabic language. The Arabs gave the moon this name because it usually appears on the horizon before sunset,[53] and by doing so takes the initiative

52 Faris, M. *How to set goals like a gardener*, [website] https://productivemuslim.com/how-to-set-goals-like-a-gardener/, last accessed December 2021.

53 Ibn Manzoor, *Lisan Al-Arab,* (Dar Sader, Beirut 1993).

in spreading its light before the day goes into complete darkness. The Islamic mindset, when it comes to known upcoming dangers and trials, teaches us to be proactive, to invest in preventative measures instead of corrective ones, and to always be aware of potential threats.

ACTION ITEMS AND FURTHER DISCUSSIONS

1. As educators, we need to channel the spiritual elements of our Islamic education towards planting careful and intentional seeds for the Hereafter. Classes and lectures about remembering death, belief in the Hereafter and the signs of the Day of Judgement should inspire workshops and programs on career planning, team building and political campaigning. We should be intentional in maintaining this holistic understanding and implementation of the Muslim faith, and not fall into keeping the dichotomy of separating spiritual and practical teachings.

2. Some hadith specify the best seeds to be planted for our journey to the Hereafter, such as:

   Abū Hurayrah (RA) reported: The Messenger of Allah, may Allah bless him and give him peace, said, 'When a human being dies, his deeds end except for three: ongoing charity, beneficial knowledge or a righteous child who prays for him.' (Muslim)

We should not read this hadith in isolation from other considerations that we take when we are planning for the major decisions in our lives: one cannot leave behind a righteous child without careful consideration of who they are going to marry! One cannot consider leaving beneficial knowledge in isolation from what books they read, courses they take, majors they choose and the information they consume on a daily basis. Finally, one cannot haphazardly leave behind a continuous charity if they do not take into consideration how they are earning that money and through what means. This hadith might be understood as a plan for the Hereafter, but it should be integrated into our plan for this worldly life, for how we earn our income, who we choose to marry and how we maintain our relationships and our lifelong endeavours in education.

3. Other hadith build on the messages in the commentary to support the concept of taking the initiative and planting seeds before other types of tribulation befall us:

   Abū Hurayrah (RA) related that the Messenger of Allah, may Allah bless him and give him peace, said, 'Hasten to perform good deeds before seven events. Are you waiting for poverty that makes you forgetful? Or wealth that burdens you? Or a debilitating disease or senility? Or an unexpected death or the False Messiah? Or is it evil from the Unseen you are waiting for? Or the Hour itself? The Hour will be bitter and terrible.' (Tirmidhī)

HADITH 37
DU'Ā' FOR MENTAL WELLBEING

عن أنس بن مالك رضى الله عنه قال: كنت أخدم رسول اللّٰه صلى الله عليه وسلم كلما نزل، فكنت أسمعه يكثر أن يقول: 'اللَّهُمَّ إِنِّي أَعُوذُ بِكَ مِنَ الْهَمِّ وَالْحَزَنِ، وَالْعَجْزِ وَالْكَسَلِ، وَالْبُخْلِ وَالْجُبْنِ ، وَضَلَعِ الدَّيْنِ، وَغَلَبَةِ الرِّجَالِ' . (البخاري)

Anas ibn Mālik said: 'I used to serve the Messenger of Allah, may Allah bless him and give him peace, whenever he travelled, and I used to hear him repeat this supplication a lot: "O Allah, I seek refuge in you from anxiety and grief, from weakness and laziness, from cowardice and miserliness, and from being overwhelmed with debt and overpowered by men."' (Bukhārī)

COMMENTARY

Life is not meant to be as easy and enjoyable as we want it to be, and human beings should expect trials and turmoil in their personal lives as well as in the life of a community:

We have created man for toil and trial. (al-Balad 90: 4)

Personal challenges, financial insecurity, and community turmoil may cause believers to fall victim to multiple emotional states and be crippled by them, preventing them from fulfilling their mission in life. While the expectation is that we strive to attain the status of a strong believer (as hadith 34 teaches), we may fall short of it because of multiple reasons (some of them being beyond our control). The Messenger of Allah, may Allah bless him and give him peace, informed us that emotional hardships, as well as physical illnesses, are a means of expiation and cleansing from our sins:

> *'No hardship, illness, anxiety, grief, harm or distress—not even the pricking of a thorn—afflicts a Muslim but that Allah will expiate some of his sins by it.'* (Bukhārī and Muslim)

The *du'ā'* at hand teaches us how to seek Allah's protection from getting consumed and paralyzed by multiple forms of psychological illnesses. This short and concise hadith encompasses eight obstacles that a Muslim might face in his or her life:

Anxiety (*al-hamm*) and grief (*al-ḥazan*): According to Ibn al-Qayyim (RA), *al-hamm* is fear of the future, especially in times of uncertainty, whereas *al-ḥazan* refers to sorrow and grief over the past. Another hadith teaches us how we should avoid excessive levels of anxiety over worldly matters, and turn our concerns towards the Hereafter:

> *Anas ibn Mālik (RA) related that the Messenger of Allah, may Allah bless him and grant him peace, said: 'Whoever is*

> *concerned about the Hereafter, Allah will place richness in his heart, bring his affairs together, and the world will come to him in full compliance. Whoever is concerned about the world, Allah will place poverty between his eyes, disorder his affairs, and he will get nothing of the world but what is decreed for him.'* (Tirmidhī)

As for dealing with the anguish from one's past, the Qur'an teaches us how our belief in Allah's wisdom and submission to His decree should help us overcome grief over past events:

> **No misfortune can happen, either in the earth or in yourselves, that was not set down in writing before We brought it into being—that is easy for God—so you need not grieve for what you miss or gloat over what you gain. God does not love the conceited, the boastful.** (al-Ḥadīd 57: 22-23)

Weakness (*al-'ajz*) and laziness (*al-kasal*): Ibn Al-Qayyim notes that *al-'ajz* refers to when someone is incapable of finding a way out of an obstacle, whereas *al-kasal* refers to when someone does not have the willpower to commit to a solution. On many occasions, laziness leads to procrastination, which results in delaying a task until one becomes weak and incapable of completing it.[54] The Muslim adoption of so-called self-help advice must not entail a bloated form of self-confidence. Rather, it should teach us to (i) humble ourselves and understand our weakness (hadith

54 Faris, M. *The Productive Muslim Du'a,* [website,] https://productivemuslim.com/the-productivemuslim-dua/, last accessed December 2021

31), (ii) have ultimate confidence in Allah's support (hadith 5), (iii) ignore self-doubt and negative emotions (hadith 34), and (iv) act in small but consistent steps (hadith 40).

Cowardice (*al-jubn*) and miserliness (*al-bukhl*): A major part of the Muslim worldview is to believe in the Unseen, and to be at peace with the fact that nothing will afflict us other than what Allah has decreed (as hadith 5 teaches). Consequently, this belief should empower us to take calculated risks, be generous and be ready to sacrifice whatever we deem valuable for the sake of Allah the Almighty:

> **Say [Prophet], 'If your fathers, sons, brothers, wives, tribes, the wealth you have acquired, the trade which you fear will decline, and the dwellings you love are dearer to you than God and His Messenger and the struggle in His cause, then wait until God brings about His punishment.' God does not guide those who break away.** (al-Tawbah 9: 24)

The burden of debt (*ḍala' al-dayn*) and overpowering by men (*ghalabat al-rijāl*): Being overcome by debt makes someone enslaved to others by choice, whereas experiencing the defeat of men involves being on the receiving end of oppression by force.[55] The concluding part of the hadith can occur on a personal level or on a community level. One can see the progression in these eight challenges starting from a person's own thoughts and concerns, and how they result in laziness and cowardice, ending up in enslaving and

55 Muhammad Abd al-Ra'uf Al-Minawi, *Fayd al-Qadir fi Sharh al-Jami' al-Saghir*, (Dat Al Marifah, Beirut, 1972).

subjugating a whole community. The Muslim community as a whole cannot reclaim its position and contribute to the world without having strong, independent, and productive members.

ACTION ITEMS AND FURTHER DISCUSSION

1. One way to fight grief and sorrow is by reframing all our sad experiences in the past, present or future, as opportunities for the expiation of sins as well as for spiritual growth. The Qur'an teaches us:

   Say, 'Only what God has decreed will happen to us. He is our Master: let the believers put their trust in God.' (al-Tawbah 9: 51)

   Linguistically speaking, the *ayah* is saying, 'no calamity will hit us except what Allah has written for us'. It is interesting that the verse did not use *'alaynā* (against us). In other words, Allah's decree, either easy or difficult in our view, is always meant to be for our growth, our learning, and our personal improvement. In their spiritual and materialistic aspects, such calamities shape our character, refine our skills and help us grow to become better stewards for Allah on Earth.

2. Muslim activists should not surrender to the victim mentality that may afflict communities that experience multiple aspects of oppression. Victims seek to shift

the blame from themselves and focus on complaining, instead of doing, they reject any advice or attempt to improve their situation. This is why the Messenger of Allah, may Allah bless him and give him peace, made sure that the Companions in the early days of Makkah did not develop such an attitude. He made sure to give them the glad tidings of Allah's help coming, while making sure that their complaints about their situation did not result in doubting Allah's help and eventually losing patience and perseverance:

Khabbāb ibn al-Arat related that we complained to the Messenger of Allah, may Allah bless him and give him peace, while he was leaning upon his cloak in the shade of the Kaaba. We said, 'Will you ask Allah to help us? Will you supplicate to Allah for us?' The Prophet said, 'Among those before you, a believer would be seized, a ditch would be dug for him, and he would be thrown into it. Then, they would bring a saw that would be put on top of his head to split him into two halves, and his flesh would be torn from the bone with iron combs. Yet, all of this did not cause him to abandon his religion. By Allah, this religion will prevail until a rider travels from Yemen to Hadramawt, fearing no one but Allah and the wolf, lest it trouble his sheep. Rather, you are being impatient.' (Bukhārī)

3. Sometimes a person may experience extreme symptoms of anxiety and depression, due to multiple factors, which could include underlying biological or genetic factors. Therefore, it is imperative for

such a person to seek help from a knowledgeable and practising Muslim therapist. Such help does not deny one's faith or connection to Allah, so long as the intervention that they seek is aligned with the Islamic paradigm of life, spirituality, morality, and mental wellbeing.[56]

HADITH 38
PROTECTION FROM BURNOUT

وعن أبي جحيفة وهب بن عبد الله رضي الله عنه قال: آخى النبي صلى الله عليه وسلم بين سلمان وأبي الدرداء ، فزار سلمان أبا الدرداء، فرأى أم الدرداء متبذلة فقال: ما شأنك قالت: أخوك أبو الدرداء ليس له حاجة في الدنيا، فجاء أبو الدرداء فصنع له طعاماً، فقال له: كل فإنى صائم، قال: ما أنا بآكل حتى تأكل، فأكل، فلما كان الليل ذهب أبو الدرداء يقوم فقال له: نم، فنام، ثم ذهب يقوم فقال له : نم، فلما كان من آخر الليل قال سلمان: قم الآن: فصليا جميعاً، فقال له سلمان: إن لربك عليك حقاً، وإن لنفسك عليك حقاً، ولأهلك عليك حقاً، فأعط كل ذى حق حقه، فأتى النبي صلى الله عليه وسلم فذكر ذلك له، فقال النبي صلى الله عليه وسلم 'صدق سلمان' (رواه البخاري).

Abū Juḥayfah related that the Prophet, may Allah bless him and give him peace, created a bond of fellowship between Salmān and Abū al-Dardā'. Salmān visited Abū al-Dardā' and found his wife Umm al-Dardā' dressed in worn-out

56 Abdallah Rothman and Adrian Coyle, (2018) 'Toward a framework for Islamic psychology and psychotherapy: An Islamic model of the soul', *Journal of Religion and Health*, 57 (2018), 1731–1744.

clothing. He asked her why she was like this. She said, 'Your brother Abū al-Dardā' is not interested in the luxuries of this world.' Then Abū al-Dardā' entered and prepared a meal for Salmān. Salmān asked Abū al-Dardā' to eat with him but he said, 'I am fasting'. Salmān said, 'I will not eat until you eat.' So Abū al-Dardā' broke his fast and ate with him. When night-time arrived, Abū al-Dardā' stood for prayer but Salmān asked him to sleep, and Abū al-Dardā' slept. After a while, Abū al-Dardā' arose again but Salmān asked him to sleep. When it was the last hours of the night, Salmān asked him to get up and they both offered the night prayer. Salmān said to him, 'You have a duty to your Lord, you have a duty to your body, and you have a duty to your family, so you should give each one its rights.' Abū al-Dardā' came to the Prophet and told him the whole story, and the Prophet, may Allah bless him and give him peace, commented, 'Salmān is correct.'

COMMENTARY

Salmān's advice in this narration is an essential reminder for community workers and activists who tend to deprioritize personal or family duties to teach a class, attend a meeting or travel for an event. It is a well-known fact that Islam teaches us to sacrifice our time, money and leisure for the sake of the community. However, such sacrifice shall not result in neglecting other responsibilities in life. We need to apply the shepherd mindset (as in hadith 11) and make sure that we tend to the flock we are responsible for.

The incident between Salmān and Abū al-Dardā' shifts the discussion from balancing family with community or worship and personal time into one of giving each duty its right. We should not be forced into a zero-sum game where we prefer one option while feeling guilty about the other. Moreover, Islam's holistic definition of worship includes many other activities, as long as they are permissible and done with the right intention. This was verified in this hadith when the Messenger of Allah, may Allah bless him and give him peace, told the Companions, may Allah be pleased with them:

> *'And in a man's intimate relations with his wife, is charity.' They said, 'O Messenger of Allah, is there a reward for one who satisfies his passions?' The Prophet said, 'You see that if he were to satisfy his passions with the unlawful, it would be a burden of sin upon him? Likewise, if he were to satisfy himself with the lawful, he will have a reward.'* (Muslim)

In other words, seeking balance in fulfilling our duties is the best way to worship Allah and closest to the Sunnah of his Messenger, may Allah bless him and give him peace:

> *Anas ibn Mālik (RA) related that some of the Companions of the Prophet, may Allah bless him and give him peace, asked the wives of the Prophet about deeds that he performed in private. Some said, 'I will not marry women.' And some said, 'I will not eat meat.' And some said, 'I will never sleep in a bed.' The Prophet praised and glorified Allah, and he said, 'What is the matter with some people who say this? I pray and I sleep, I fast*

> *and I break fasting, and I marry women. Whoever does not desire my Sunnah is not part of me.'* (Muslim)

Ibn al-Qayyim has a beautiful commentary where he says:

> For every command that Allah has given, Satan will try to send it into one of two extremes: either complete abandonment and neglect (*tafrīṭ*), or to overzealousness and excessive application (*ifrāṭ*). The religion of Allah is meant to stay on the moderate path between those who neglect its commands and those who are fanatical about them.[57]

It is very important, when discussing balance, that we understand Salman's advice and put it in context. The discussion was about voluntary prayers and fasting not affecting his relationship with his wife and his family. Balance should not become an invitation to abandon the obligatory (*farḍ*) commands of the faith, such as the five daily prayers, modest clothing for men and women and staying away from the impermissible.

57 Ibn al-Qayyim, *Madārij al-Sālikīn*.

ACTION ITEMS AND FURTHER DISCUSSIONS

1. Reflect on the following prophetic advice on setting long-term goals, and ensuring sustainability and consistency in our deeds, habits, activities, education and programs: 'The traveller who pushes his animal faster than its capacity will not reach his destination, nor will he be able to use it for future journeys.' (hadith, rated as weak in transmission)

2. Our responsibilities towards our community and our involvement in public activities should not become an excuse to escape from well-known duties, especially towards our immediate family members:

   Believers, guard yourselves and your families against a Fire fuelled by people and stones. (al-Taḥrīm 66: 6)

   It might be easier to preach at the mosque or teach other people's kids than your own. However, the real challenge and the real impact come when we give our attention to our family members, even those who might disagree completely with us. We should not lose sight of the strong emphasis in Islam on keeping ties of kinship, as in the hadith: *"'Ā'ishah reported that the Messenger of Allah, may Allah bless him and give him peace, said, "The bond of family is suspended from the Throne and it says: Whoever upholds me, Allah will uphold him. Whoever severs me, Allah will sever him."'* (Bukhārī)

3. The balance taught by this hadith was hard to maintain even among the Companions, may Allah be pleased with them. Some of them felt guilty about the times when they felt less spiritual or became distracted from the Hereafter with worldly enjoyments.

   Ḥanẓalah reported that he asked: O Messenger of Allah, when we are in your presence and are reminded of Hellfire and Paradise, we feel as if we are seeing them with our very eyes, but when we leave you and attend to our wives, our children, and our business, most of these things slip from our minds. The Prophet replied, By Him in whose hand is my soul, if your state of mind remains the same as it is in my presence and you are always occupied with the remembrance of Allah, the angels will shake your hands in your beds and roads. O Ḥanẓalah, rather time should be devoted to this and time should be devoted to that. (Muslim)

HADITH 39
FINANCIAL INDEPENDENCE

عن أبي هريرة عن النبي صلى الله عليه وسلم أنه قال: 'اليد العليا خير من اليد السفلى وابدأ بمن تعول، وخير الصدقة ما كان عن ظهر غنًى، ومن يستعفف، يعفه الله، ومن يستغن، يغنه الله' (رواه البخاري).

> *The Prophet, may Allah bless him and give him peace, said: 'The upper hand (that gives) is better than the lower one (that receives). Make sure to give those who are under your care first, and the best charity is that which is given out of surplus; and whoever abstains from the unlawful, Allah will support him in his abstinence, and whoever seeks financial independence, Allah will make him self-sufficient.'* (Bukhārī)

COMMENTARY

In a similar fashion to the other hadith in this chapter, this narration changes the narrative on wealth, teaching that it is not a means to fulfil one's ego and desires, but to plant seeds for the Hereafter and benefit one's family and community. The bare minimum of requirements is to not be a burden on others:

> *'No food is better for you than what is earned through your own labour. Verily, the Prophet Dāwūd only used to eat from the fruits of his own hands.'* (Bukhārī)

The hadith emphasizes that providing for those under our custody takes higher priority over other charitable acts. Any discussion on sacrificing a materialistic life and implementing asceticism (*zuhd*) before ensuring that one's dependents are self-sufficient goes against the proper Islamic understanding of wealth and spirituality:

> *'A person cannot be more sinful than the one who deprives those under his care from their food and sustenance.'* (Muslim)

In addition, this important principle holds true for leaders, organizations and communities. Muslim scholars and leaders cannot maintain their independent positions and fulfil their roles in enjoining good and forbidding evil while being dependent on a salary. This is where utilizing Islamic charitable endowments (*awqāf*)[58] is essential to ensure that the intellectual integrity of scholars is protected. When speaking about the Muslim community at large, our mission as caretakers of this earth cannot be fulfilled if we remain as a burden on the world. The *ummah* of the Messenger who was sent as a mercy to mankind, may Allah bless him and give him peace, needs to adopt this mindset wholeheartedly: to become the upper hand that creates jobs and pushes the economy forward, the innovative mind that finds solutions to today's challenges, and the heart that cares about others.

FURTHER DISCUSSIONS

1. As a community, we need to integrate our charitable work with our *da'wah* and educational messaging in the light of this hadith. This ensures that our charity is not spent in ways that create a life-long dependency of the needy on it. We should promote the *fiqh* of financial independence (*ta'affuf*) as much

58 https://yaqeeninstitute.org/khalil-abdurrashid/financing-kindness-as-a-society-the-rise-fall-of-islamic-philanthropic-institutions-waqfs

as we promote the *fiqh* of charity and donation, otherwise we will be hurting the same people we are trying to help. The following story, narrated by Anas ibn Mālik (RA), highlights the Prophet's approach in helping people become self-sufficient:

A man from the Anṣār came to the Messenger of Allah, may Allah bless him and give him peace, and asked for some provisions. The Prophet Muhammad, may Allah bless him and give him peace, asked, 'Do you have anything to sell in your house?' The main replied, 'Yes, a cloth—we wear some of it and spread the rest on the ground, and a wooden bowl from which we drink water.' The Prophet said, 'Bring them to me.'

So, after the man brought them in, the Messenger of Allah, may Allah bless him and give him peace, held them and asked, 'Who will buy these?'

A man said, 'I will buy them for one dirham.' And the Messenger repeated two or three times: 'Who will offer more than a dirham?'

A man said, 'I will buy them for two dirhams.' So the Prophet took the two dirhams and gave them to the man, then he said, 'Buy food with one of them for your family and buy an axe with the other one and come to me.'

He then brought it to him, and the Prophet, may Allah bless him and give him peace, fixed a handle on it with his own hands and said, 'Go gather firewood and sell it, and I shall not see you for the next fifteen days.'

The man went away to chop and sell wood, and eventually earned ten dirhams. He came to the Messenger after buying a garment and food for his family. The Prophet, may Allah bless him and give him peace, then said: 'What you did is much better than being resurrected on the Day of Judgement with a spot on your face due to asking for money from others. Indeed, requesting money is only allowed for three: for those under grinding poverty, or those in severe debt, or for those who need to compensate for blood money.' (Abū Dāwūd, rated as good (*ḥasan*) in transmission)

2. Amongst the Companions of the Messenger of Allah, may Allah be pleased with them, we have the great example of ʿAbd al-Raḥmān ibn ʿAwf (RA) as the embodiment of this hadith. He was amongst the wealthiest businessmen in Makkah, but that did not stop him from being one of the many men to accept Islam. Moreover, when he migrated to Madinah, he sacrificed all of his wealth and proved that the pursuit of wealth did not affect his decision. In Madinah, he was partnered with Saʿd ibn al-Rabīʿ (RA) who offered to share half of his wealth with him, but instead he said, 'Show me where the marketplace is.' Despite starting over from scratch, he was able to build up immense wealth, which enabled him to support the Muslim community

further. Ṭalhah narrated that most of the citizens of Madinah depended on ʿAbd al-Raḥmān: one third were employed by him, one third had their loans covered by him and one third received some form of charity from him.[59]

3. As community members who always strive to make a difference, we need to find multiple ways to support ourselves and our families through passive income, such as investing. This should help us to free up the most important asset a believer has, which is his or her time! Just imagine how much benefit a Muslim might be able to bring in his or her active time if it wasn't for the daily grind needed to make a living. We should strive to follow through the example of ʿAbd al-Raḥmān ibn ʿAwf and allow our wealth to enable multiple facets of good, so long as we keep our intentions sincere and our actions aligned with what Allah and His Messenger approves.

59 Al-Dhahabī, *Siyar Aʿlām al-Nubalāʾ*.

HADITH 40
SMALL DEEDS LIKE THE CONSISTENT RAIN

عن عائشة رضي الله عنها قالت: سئل النبي صلى الله عليه و سلم: أي الأعمال أحب إلى الله؟ قال: أدومها وإن قل وقال اكلفوا من الأعمال ما تطيقون.
(البخاري)

'Ā'ishah narrates that the Prophet, may Allah bless him and give him peace, was asked about the most beloved deeds to Allah, and he answered, 'The most consistent ones even if they are few in number.' He also said, 'Commit to the deeds you can sustain.' (Bukhārī)

COMMENTARY

The last hadith in this collection provides an important reminder when trying to put into practice the other hadith mentioned above. Allah expects consistency from us—He appreciates when these small deeds turn into habits, and when our bursts of motivation become anchors of steadfastness in our faith:

> **O you who believe, be patient, act with discipline, guard your frontlines and fear Allah, so that you may be successful.** (āl 'Imrān 3: 200)

Human beings tend to be seasonal in the way they carry themselves in life. There is a season for shopping, another for taking a holiday and yet another to study or work. Similarly, there is a season where our faith and spirituality are at their highest (as in Ramadan); however, this should not result in slacking off completely during the remaining months of the year, by abandoning fundamental practices completely like prayer, for example. It is true that we should encourage people to get closer to Allah all year round by doing more, but we should also strive for consistency and steadfastness. 'Ā'ishah, may Allah be pleased with her, was asked if the Messenger of Allah, may Allah bless him and give him peace, would dedicate certain deeds for certain days, and she answered, *'No, for his deeds were consistent, but who amongst you can tolerate what the Messenger of Allah, may Allah bless him and give him peace, tolerated.'* (Bukhārī)

It is interesting that 'Ā'ishah used the word *dima* to describe the Messenger's consistent deeds. In the Arabic language, this refers to the cloud that drops rain consistently for days. In a sense, this hadith describes that his deeds had both consistency, quality, quantity and a goal that clearly none of us can achieve!

This hadith should inspire us to build our activities, programmes and institutions around consistent but impactful work:

- Recurring classes and educational events should be given more importance over bigger but occasional events.
- Grassroot work and local campaigning that mobilise our communities should be given priority over any bigger rallies or events.
- Establishing deep and meaningful relationships with all segments of society, especially those who disagree with us, should be the basis of our outreach, in addition to

issuing a press statement or raising awareness through an outreach event.

A community, like an individual, requires consistency, gradual steps, and continuous education in order to heal, empower, and educate its members and advance their situation.

FURTHER DISCUSSIONS AND ACTION ITEMS

1. This hadith should not be taken out of context to justify mediocrity in worship and community work. We should strive to bring out the best that Muslim community members can offer. The main message that is manifested in the order of the words suggests that we should direct our willpower, determination, and ambition towards consistency. After highlighting this command very clearly, the Prophet's words indicated that the size of the deed does not matter, so long as the deed itself is persistent. The encouragement to hold on firmly to the teachings of Islam is reiterated in multiple places in the Qur'an, such as in Allah's command to Prophet Yaḥya, may Allah give him peace:

   'Yaḥya, hold on to the Scripture firmly.' While he was still a boy, We granted him wisdom. (Maryam 19: 12)

2. Consistency should manifest itself in other areas of our activism, such as giving different causes of

suffering and injustice their due (refer to hadith 27). It should also guide the way we react to natural disasters and calamities to donate in an educated and responsible manner, not out of pure emotion. Excessive donations pouring into one location may open the door for corruption and misuse of such donations. Certain countries and causes can become neglected just because they seem to be less urgent in the eyes of the masses than the one experiencing an urgent crisis.

3. One of the best ways to encourage consistency is to demonstrate its impact. For example, if you calculate how much you can memorize of the Qur'an by sticking to a few lines per day or one page per week, in addition to a consistent revision schedule?[60] Interestingly enough, such an estimate could even underestimate the real impact, since consistency creates competency, which will increase the speed and the quality of the memorization as the days pass.

60 Hani, S., *114 Tips to Help You Finally Memorize the Qur'an*, (CreateSpace Independent Publishing Platform, 2016).

CONCLUDING REMARKS

THANK YOU FOR taking the time to navigate the 40 hadith on community service and activism. As indicated earlier, this collection is only meant to serve as a discussion starter into this ever-evolving topic, and as a Muslim handbook to change the world. It provides the hadith that answer the most important questions about a Muslim's involvement in this space. These questions may be summarized as follows:

CHAPTER ONE
THE WHY: THE SPIRITUAL MOTIVATION OF AN ACTIVIST

The hadith in this chapter invite us to begin every act of service with the very end in mind—with reflection on the moment we meet our Lord on the Day of Judgement. The spiritual element of activism invites us to revisit our intentions before, during, and after our community work (hadith 1). It encourages us to work behind the scenes (hadith 2) while protecting ourselves from the detrimental effects of stinginess and desires (hadith 3). Keeping Allah at the centre of our goals and aspirations invites us to serve His creation, since the most beloved servants to Allah are the ones who are the most beneficial to His creation (hadith 4). It also provides the spiritual motivation to stay strong and courageous during tough times (hadith 5) and to not be discouraged by the overwhelming prevalence of falsehood (hadith 6).

CHAPTERS TWO AND THREE
THE WHAT: THE SOCIAL & POLITICAL RESPONSIBILITIES OF MUSLIM ACTIVISTS

The hadith in Chapter 2 provide guidance on *What* is expected from Muslims as vicegerents of God on earth: hadith 7 teaches us to spread peace, feed the hungry, keep our ties of kinship, without forgetting about our spiritual connection with Allah through night prayers. Hadith 8 describes the branches of the tree of faith, from testifying to the Oneness of Allah to good manners and modesty to eventually removing harm from the streets. Hadith 9 reminds us that all of us are responsible for our flock, and empowers us to work within our circles of influence. Hadith 11 warns us from abandoning our duties as reformers, since Islam views the society as a single ship (hadith 12), where the actions of sinners and wrongdoers affect all human beings, and thus the importance of taking responsibility and action.

Moving on to Chapter 3 where the hadith about a Muslim's service to society in the political spheres are discussed. Hadith 12 gives the famous prophetic command to change any wrongdoing that we encounter with one's hand, tongue, or heart. Hadith 13 indicates how the higher form of Jihad is to speak truth to power. Hadith 14 shows the prophetic wisdom on being strategic and choosing our battles on what evil things we should prioritize. Hadith 15 emphasizes a Muslim's positive interaction with other cultures while they navigate the political circles, without completely dismissing positive values or compromising their principles. A Muslim's attention to the media and public image is highlighted in hadith 16 by narrating the story of Ḥassān the poet and his service to the Muslim community. This chapter is concluded with a much-needed advice in hadith 17 that challenges how we think about our political parties and affiliations, and invites us to support the side of truth, even if it meant to go against our own brethren.

CHAPTER FOUR
THE WHO: INSIDE YOUR TEAM
PROPHETIC WISDOM ON EMPOWERING AND LEADING A SUCCESSFUL TEAM

The hadith in Chapter 4 are meant to guide our organizations and teams on the best practices to operate a team, all from prophetic advice. Hadith 18 starts with declaring the scarcity of dependable leaders and volunteers and invites us to value and appreciate the ones who work with us more. Hadith 19 warns us from materialistic standards penetrating our organizations. Hadith 20 answers to some level of detail whether it is permissible for a team member to nominate themselves for a leadership position. Working within teams can create backlash, but this should not cause us to resort to isolation and quit on attempts to work with our people (hadith 21). Hadith 22 gives an insight, through the story of the *Adhān*, the recruiting methodology that Prophet Muhammad, may Allah bless him and give him peace, used and how he assigned tasks to different community members. This chapter is concluded with hadith 23, which discusses the dynamics of *Shūrā* and discipline between team members and their leadership.

CHAPTERS FIVE AND SIX
THE HOW: THE ADAB & *FIQH* OF ACTIVISM

Chapter 5 discusses the code of conduct that guides *How* Muslims should carry themselves while fulfilling their duties, firstly towards Allah and then towards their community. Hadith 24 teaches about sincere goodwill (*Naṣīḥah*) as a core value in Islam and how giving advice should be present in a community's life. Hadith 25 gives the etiquette of receiving and sharing news, and the importance of verifying our sources of information. Hadith 26 introduces excellence *(Iḥsān)* as the DNA of a Muslim's work ethics and hadith 27 emphasizes brotherhood and unity between the different members of a community through the beautiful imagery of the bricks that belong to the same structure. The chapter concludes with hadith 28 on dealing with people in a prophetic way, especially our neighbours and guests.

Chapter 6 brings an important aspect to the *How* question by providing hadith that discuss the boundaries of permissibility in activism work (the *halal* and the *ḥarām*). Hadith 29 weighs in on the Islamic moral view on the end versus the means question, while hadith 30 reminds us of the complexity of issues where the defining line between the *ḥalāl* and the *ḥarām* is not clear. Hadith 31 compliments this discussion by inviting a Muslim to work within their capacity and avoid a perfectionist, all-or-nothing mentality. Hadith 32 on the treaty of *al-Fuḍūl* builds the case for collaborating with non-Muslim groups on matters of shared benefit. The chapter concludes with hadith 33 on the guidance to handle differences of opinion, especially when it comes to different ways of interpreting and applying our Muslim sacred text.

CHAPTER SEVEN
THE WHILE: GUIDE FOR SELF-CARE AND PROTECTION FROM BURNOUT

Chapter 7 is meant to conclude the book with prophetic wisdom to inspire Muslim activists and tend to their mental wellbeing. This is much-needed advice, given the fact that most community volunteers and workers are known to be selfless and generous with almost everything they have. They always put others before themselves and go out of their way to serve their organizations, but this normally comes at what is commonly referred to as volunteer burnout.

Hadith 34 encourages the believers to invest in self-development and work towards the goal of being the strong believer, while hadith 35 warns against pessimism and negativity when we do not see results of our work. Such resilience can be achieved by having a mindset of planting seeds wherever we go (hadith 36) even if the Day of Judgement is about to start. Hadith 37 gives a beautiful *Du'ā'* for mental wellbeing that helps Muslim activists conquer that internal battle from within their hearts. Hadith 38 shows how Islam encourages us not to prioritize community work over other responsibilities, especially health and family. Hadith 39 stresses the importance of financial independence so we can strengthen our position in society while pleasing Allah the almighty. Hadith 40 concludes the book on the importance of maintaining small consistent deeds, for the change we all desire will not happen overnight.

As we come towards the end of our journey of the 40 hadith on community service and activism, it is essential to summarize the central themes and underlying messages that every Muslim activist should learn, agree on, and strive towards implementing into their worldview and eventually their activism. These could serve as a manifesto that would then always be present in our organizations, meetings, and *tarbiyah* framework.

THE MUSLIM ACTIVIST MANIFESTO

1. Real change can only come from Allah. It is He who puts *barakah*, spiritual blessings and aid and support, into the little work that we do and brings the best outcome out of it, both in the hereafter (which is our priority) as well as the worldly life (as a side benefit):

   Whoever seeks honour and power, then let them know that all honour and power belongs to Allah. To Him alone good words ascend, and righteous deeds are raised up by Him. (Fāṭir 35:10)

   It is Allah alone who brings out the best outcome from every seed we plant. It is Allah alone who can make it stay, thrive, and benefit more people.

   Consider the seeds you sow in the ground, is it you who make them grow or We? If We wished, We could turn your harvest into chaff and leave

you to wail, 'We are burdened with debt; rather we are totally deprived.' (al-Wāqiʿah 56: 63-67)

And on the same token, it is Allah alone who weeds out the noise, and makes what is hype and popular but insincere, go away, wither and eventually become forgotten:

As for the froth of the sea, it disappears, but that which benefits people remains in the earth. (al-Raʿd 13:17)

2. God consciousness (*Taqwa*) is a pre-requisite for any deed to be accepted. Muslims should seek the acceptance from Allah first and foremost before any of His creation:

   Relate to them in truth O Prophet the story of Adam's two sons—how each offered a sacrifice: Abel's offering was accepted while Cain's was not. So Cain threatened, 'I will kill you!' His brother replied, 'Allah only accepts the offering of the sincerely devout. (Al-Mā'idah 5:27)

3. As Muslims, our morality and our standards of what is right and what is wrong are defined by God. They are not relative to every generation or every community's whim and desire. We firmly believe in the absolute knowledge and wisdom of the One who created us and knows what is right for us in our worldly matters as well as matters of the hereafter:

How could He not know His Own creation? For He alone is the Most Subtle, All-Aware. (al-Mulk 67:14)

This is why having good intentions *has* to be accompanied by following the correct path according to Islamic principles, which is the path of Prophet Muhammad (may Allah bless him and give him peace):

Say, [O Muhammad], 'If you should love Allah, then follow me, [so] Allah will love you and forgive you your sins. And Allah is Forgiving and Merciful.' (*Āl 'Imrān* 3:31)

4. The so-called 'worldly affairs' are inseparable from spiritual ones in Islam. The rituals for a Muslim, such as the five daily prayers, are meant to guide our day-to-day actions. Allah the almighty criticized the community of Prophet Shuʿayb, may Allah send him peace, when they rejected the interference of the religion into their business transactions:

   They said, 'Shuʿayb, does your prayer tell you that we should abandon what our forefathers worshiped and refrain from doing whatever we please with our own wealth? Indeed, you are a tolerant and sensible man. (Hūd 11:87)

This is why our Islamic approach towards community service, both in the social and political spheres, is a part of a holistic understanding of worship to Allah in all matters of our lives. We don't pick and choose from the religion what fits our agenda and platform, but rather use the entire teachings of Islam as the guiding principles for our activism:

O believers! Enter into Islam wholeheartedly and do not follow Satan's footsteps. Surely he is your sworn enemy. (al-Baqarah 2:208)

5. Muslim activists should avoid, by any means, the attempts to compromise certain aspects of their faith while attempting to navigate modern day challenges and representing Islam's position. The Qur'an warns us from speaking on behalf of Allah without any knowledge, and listed such action among other major sins:

   Say, 'My Lord has only forbidden open and secret indecencies, sinfulness, unjust aggression, associating others with Allah in worship—a practice He has never authorized—and attributing to Allah what you do not know.' (al-A'rāf 7:33)

   Similarly, Allah summons Prophet Muhammad, may Allah bless him and give him peace, as well as his community, to deliver the message of the Qur'an and not be ashamed of any element of it:

This is a Book sent down to you, O Prophet—do not let anxiety into your heart regarding it—so with it you may warn the disbelievers, and as a reminder to the believers. (al-A'rāf 7:2)

6. Islam's solution to racism and inequality can be summarized by the statement of Rub'ī ibn 'Āmir, the Companion who told Rustum, the commander of the Persian army:

   Allah sent us as ambassadors to liberate people from being enslaved to other people to true servitude to Allah, the Lord of all people, and from the tightness of the worldly life to the vastness of the world and the hereafter, and from the injustice of other religions to the justice brought by Islam. [61]

   In Islam, *taqwā* is the only criteria that matters in the eyes of Allah the Almighty, aside from any ethnic, social, racial or financial measures:

   O humanity! Indeed, We created you from a male and a female, and made you into peoples and tribes so that you may get to know one another. Surely the most noble of you in the sight of Allah

61 Ibn Kathir, *Al-Bidayah Wa Al-Nihaya*, vol 9, p.619 (Beirut : Dar al-Kutub al-Ilmiya, 1988).

is the most righteous among you. Allah is truly All-Knowing, All-Aware. (al-Ḥujurāt 49:13)

7. The call for social justice in Islam is tightly connected to the call for *Tawḥīd* (affirming the Oneness of Allah). This was the mission of all messengers before Prophet Muhammad, may Allah bless them and give them all peace:

   Indeed, We sent Our messengers with clear proofs, and with them We sent down the Scripture and the balance of justice so that people may administer justice. And We sent down iron with its great might, benefits for humanity, and means for Allah to prove who is willing to stand up for Him and His messengers without seeing Him. Surely Allah is All-Powerful, Almighty. (al-Ḥadid 57:25)

   Likewise, the Muslim community is commanded to follow through that legacy, and establish justice between all, regardless of people's religion or faith:

   Indeed, Allah commands you to return trusts to their rightful owners; and when you judge between people, judge with fairness. What a noble commandment from Allah to you! Surely Allah is All-Hearing, All-Seeing. (al-Nisā' 4:58)

Do not let the hatred of a people who once barred you from the Sacred Mosque provoke you to transgress. (al-Mā'idah 5:2)

8. Activism and community service are modern day manifestations of the Qur'anic commandment of enjoining good and forbidding evil.

   Let there be a group among you who call 'others' to goodness, encourage what is good, and forbid what is evil—it is they who will be successful. (āl 'Imrān 3:104)

   The Qur'an narrates multiple stories of messengers and prophets who had both the missions of *da'wah* as well as speaking truth to power. Prophet Mūsā called the Pharaoh to the worship of Allah:

   Speak to him gently, so perhaps he may be mindful 'of Me or fearful of My punishment.' (Ṭa-Ha 20:44)

   In addition, Mūsā and Hārūn strived to stop the oppression from Banū Isrā'īl:

   Let the Children of Israel go with us. (al-Shuarā' 26:17)

9. Muslim community workers should strive towards unity and keep their co-operation and collaboration

to achieve the best results that please Allah the Almighty:

Co-operate with one another in goodness and righteousness, and do not co-operate in sin and transgression (al-Mā'idah 5:2)

Obey Allah and His Messenger and do not dispute with one another, or you would be discouraged and weakened. Persevere! Surely Allah is with those who persevere. (al-Anfāl 8:46)

10. Muslim activists and leaders should follow the example of Prophet Muhammad, peace and blessings be upon him, in maintaining the highest character and manners:

And you are truly a man of outstanding character. (al-Qalam 68:4)

The Qur'an praised the messenger of Allah, may Allah bless him and give him peace, for maintaining such an attitude even in the most difficult situations, such as the battle of Uḥud:

It is out of Allah's mercy that you O Prophet have been lenient with them. Had you been cruel or hard-hearted, they would have certainly abandoned you. (āl 'Imrān 3:159)